THE AFRICAN NARRATIVE

S. NAMOUZ

.2018

BLANK

FOREWORD

"None are more hopelessly enslaved than those who falsely believe they are free"

Johann Wolfgang von Goethe, 1749-1832

Who is man? Is it just another animal with the ability to think and reason? To think meaning to recognize your past, present and potential circumstances, and to fashion out ways of resolving them; and to reason being to use the mental faculties bestowed on man to build a self-sustaining environment to ensure his wellbeing. So the primary objective of man is to survive by way of thinking and reasoning. And this, He has done since the dawn of time. Long ago in the precarious jungles of Africa when man first walked the earth, every sunrise was a new day for him to get through by hunting and gathering small pockets of food with constant innovation and adaptability; most of his actions for his own betterment and survival were at the expense of lower animals and weaker men — some of whom are now extinct. In the final analysis; only the fittest survives.

As time went by, it became necessary to form alliances in order to stay safe and ultimately, increase longevity. Living in solitude was not an option for the early man and evidently, for the modern man as well. This simple survival concept would later become the basis for nations, kingdoms and empires to emerge all over the world. Humans, they say are social beings — meaning humans depend on the association with one another to live, develop and thrive. So important is the need to affiliate, that it is only second to our need to live, i.e. food, air and shelter according to Abraham Maslow, in his Needs Pyramid theory.

It would seem that man was afflicted with some kind of impulse that involuntarily impels us to belong with others and makes living in solitude so difficult. If a person lives in solitude for too long, scientists tell us they develop psychological disorders. This is the natural way of bringing communities together and organizing them into human institutions. Simply put, humanity needs social galvanization to bloom. And yet, it is society that also presents the most danger to a person because so far as we know, a goat would not **conspire** with your dog to murder you. It is only your fellow man who has that ability.

In the earliest times, man traversed far and wide in pursuit of his quest for survival. Some more daring and dauntless than others, and some more reasonable than others. All of this demonstrates the various levels of the use of our mental faculties. Natural selection and mechanisms dispersed man across the earth; each according to his ability and due, to our present settlements. Nonetheless, no one continent can claim superiority over the other either in terms of its populations or natural resources. The oceans did their best to divide the various lands accordingly. And all peoples of the world ought to be proud of who they are, where they are placed and what they have.

We may say that those men who managed to escape Africa into other territories for survival were truly remarkable, intelligent and brave to have devised transportation to other lands. We may also say that, those men who remained in Africa were equally profound in the use of their abilities to tame their treacherous environment to build their home. Therefore, let us not make a fundamental mistake to judge that some are more gifted than others. And whether, melanin has a positive or negative correlation with Intelligence is a matter for further scientific enquiry. What we know now is that all men have equal organismic make-up, save the color.

The development and evolution of man from antiquity until now, as I have observed, have been along the lines of self-preservation, greed and dominion. And why not, since our most basic instinct is survival? Values such as compassion, generosity and the rest are acquired traits through environmental and social conditioning. That is, it is not in the nature of man to show compassion or be magnanimous. But we accept and cherish those values because without them there will be no harmony.

Self-preservation can be seen as a manifestation of our innate desire to look after our own before that of others. In a life threatening situation our first impulse will be to flee to safety and if possible help others to escape as well but the first duty is always to the self. However, when people exhibit this instinct more than acceptable or reasonable, then they're described in a negative sense - selfishness.

It's been said that the only people who would want you to surpass their accomplishment are your parents (such a selfless wish) - but even then, this is not all truly altruistic, because a successful child could mean a comfortable retirement for the parent. It is as if we can find some selfish motive for every action a person takes if we look hard enough.

This, however, is not tantamount to being self-indulgent; It is taking reasonable steps or decisions in your own favor which otherwise might lead to the annihilation of your life or some critical personal value; which is vital to your livelihood and person. So self-preservation can be dispensed without unduly taking advantage of others. Self-preservation is a form of selfishness and that doctrine can be applied to other spheres of life not necessarily the protection of one's existence. On a daily basis we all take decisions that inherently, benefits just the self.

Greed, stems from man's inborn desire for economic freedom and security. In our quest to meet our basic needs. We build up so much fear about the future and about the needs of those we care for such that we always want to amass as much as we can to guarantee our security.

Therefore, the more we have the more our fears abate. But when we exercise this drive more than necessary, in every little opportunity, fair or unfair, then the negative description of greed is placed on us.

Dominion over others, be it fellow men or lower creatures is what assures the perpetuation of the earlier traits discussed above. Because when we dominate over others, we can use them to meet our selfish desires and to produce enough to guarantee our security.

Self-preservation, greed and dominion are very natural and normal and are not peculiar to a particular region or people but all human beings. Right here in Africa, before the arrival of the white man, tribes arouse against each other to subdue and rule. Slavery had long existed amongst ourselves before the white man came. So to man; love those who are closest to you, i.e. kindred and use those who are not to ensure your survival and comfort; a basic principle that permeates millennia of human existence.

First the means of sustenance formed the basis for the development of human societies, in the fullness of time, humans felt (or the circumstances demanded) the need to cement their societies together through more sentimental and solemn means. Human cultures all over the world begun to conceptualize divinity in many forms. And thus, the birth of religion.

For without something more than sustenance, a human society cannot hold for much longer. Because if one belongs to a society on account of his need for sustenance, he or she can simply move on to the next society that may provide something better. But no, human societies were built on something higher, something cosmic. Which is why no matter our present circumstances and places of abode, we always feel connected to our original society, even if sentimentally.

After the fall of the great kingdoms of Africa, i.e. ancient Egypt, Kush, Nubia, etc. the land of Africa has since been beleaguered with a chain of forces more powerful and resourceful than anything it has ever had to deal with. One that rewrites its past, manipulates its present and controls its future. There was a time, not so long though, when the white man's rhetoric about the black man was not palatable at all; that the black man was inferior race fit for only one purpose — exploitation. But although the rhetoric has changed of late, the mentality has not. And whose fault is it? I hope you remember the discussion on the nature of man above? It answers this. Because weakness invites a domineering entity to conquer.

For a very long time, the white man, not just the Europeans but including other races who hold such repugnant opinions of the black man have somehow succeeded in conditioning some Africans to believe that these opinions are indeed facts. But whether perceptions or facts, we must acknowledge that perception can be more vital than fact if the one receiving the short-end of the stick behaves in a manner that confirms the perception. I am sad to say not many Africans dare to compose themselves as to disprove this obnoxious perception of the black man. Africans but especially the leaders have given so much impression to confirm the perceptions held by the other races.

The fact that man first lived in Africa is by no accident or mistake. The earliest civilizations begun here in Africa because this land provided the basis for the development of a civilization. The resources for agriculture and food production were and still are abundant in Africa which boosted economic activities and societies erupted in large numbers. Till date Africa has given evidence of its enormous resources and potential but what has happened to all that?

It is indeed a complex situation and to understand some of these things, we need to apply resourceful thinking.

Judging by the shenanigans of the white man during the colonial era, we may say that he is very explorative, materialistic and domineering. And to date, we can only say that he has doubled in this regard. Scarcity of resources in the world has led every nation to be very competitive in order to build a sound economy for its citizens, to ensure its security and establishments. The white man too has the right to do so and does not owe any amount of compassion or pity to anyone. This is simply the crude way of seeing it, taking into consideration the historical development of human thought and the fact that we have not changed much in the ways we acquire sustenance.

After the colonization of Africa, the Trans-Atlantic Slave Trade, the world wars, the Cold War and their related economic shake-ups - the world fashioned out itself into various power blocs and alliances with the United States emerging as a unipolar superpower. This restructuring of the world occurred at a time when Africa was too powerless to participate in any high level negotiations and therefore became a bounty which was divvied up by European powers and till date, remains woefully so.

When Dr. Kwame Nkrumah of blessed memory returned from America to oil the wheels of the independence struggle of Ghana, he, like many of his compatriots believed that Africans ought to claim their right to self-determination. The feeling of self-governance had swept across Africa and other colonized territories all over the world and its realization had been vehemently pursued. This was so because there is dignity in self-rule and also because nobody can look after your interests better than yourself.

In Africa, particularly Ghana, the question I find most profound is how the infantile nation was going to manage its own affairs given its very high tribal diversity. Plus, Ghana like most African nations comprise a host of traditional political structures and a number of acephalous societies. The white man had done the groundwork by bringing all these tribes and kingdoms under the umbrella of the nation of Gold Coast (Ghana).

However, it still remained a contentious matter — how to dissolve the previous traditional political units and ethnicities at both the ideological and functional levels into the larger whole and maintaining its harmony and integrity thereafter and especially in the absence of the British colonial government.

It is difficult for a nation without patriotic countrymen to develop, therefore it was imperative for the founding body politic of African nations to have taken the bull by the horns to cast aside tribalism, which was the order of the day, and put in its stead a holistic national approach and of course, without losing sight of our rich cultural heritage. But evidently, this was poorly done considering the fact that majority of the earlier political parties were along tribal and regional lines, and have virtually remained so even now.

The situation is indeed worrisome. Patriotism is fundamentally loyalty to the State in which one is co-opted into from birth, therefore when the allegiance to the State is circumvented by sectionalism, be it tribe, party politics, trade or profession and what have you, that State actually tethers on the brink of becoming a failed state. A failed state is a country whose government institutions, particularly, political and economic, have lost the gumption to undertake their obligations and promulgate the aspirations of its people. But before a nation's institutions fail, the symptoms are enough to bring on, untold hardship and future uncertainties for the people.

It is therefore clear that without absolute loyalty to the State, there can be no common purpose in its governance. It is the commonality of purpose that underpins the workings of all State institutions, this in turn exacts confidence from the people who, individually, are the elementary instruments of the nation. This simple concept is what gives oxygen to the social contract. But when this commonality of purpose is adulterated by corruption proclivities; the State's institutions fail.

This narrative is to look at where we have come from and where we are, vis-a-vis where we want to go — as well as how to get there. It is a taskmaster indeed and cannot be done effectively without contextualizing the discussions within the framework of human behavior. This is why I earlier observed the three drivers of human behavior, i.e. self-preservation, greed and dominion.

THE COLONISTS

Take a minute to picture the boundary of the nation of Ghana. Try in your mind's eye to reverse time to a period when Accra, was but a coastal town with no tarred roads, no electricity; just a few scattered mud houses and a handful of people and a lot of trees. In this exercise, you are likely to see the *Wulormei* leading a bunch of people through various footpaths and springing *Kpokpoe* to mark the *Homowo* festival. Do the same for all the major cities that boast of millions of residents along the coast today, what do you see?

On an ordinary day, people would have been busy with farming, attending to their livestock, working in the mines and other industries of their time and even a few recreational beach users flapping themselves up and down in the Atlantic Ocean. It would have also been possible to see a few foreign people, particularly traders who traversed the many trade routes across Africa, e.g. traders from Timbuktu, Gao, Djenne, Marrakesh, Tunis, Cairo and other Saharan cities. If you were an avid observer, you might have seen a royal bursar or a business magnate sitting comfortably in his shed collecting the proceeds from his enterprise. Life was simply adequate for their time.

Prince Henry the Navigator, who was the Duke of Viseu, Portugal, is the man who defied the superstition about seafaring beyond Cape Bajador which was the southernmost point Europeans had reached on the western Saharan coast of the Atlantic before the advent of Prince Henry. He sponsored many sailors, many died but eventually they mastered the waters and colonized the territories they came in contact with. This feat enriched Portugal beyond measure and endeared the Prince to his people.

The success of Portugal caught the appetite of other Europeans who followed suit and the Scramble for Africa started and life would never be the same afterwards for Africans.

What begun in Lisbon, Portugal, under the auspices of Prince Henry the Navigator as an explorative trade mission to East Asia, by circumventing Africa had stumbled on this peaceful and gold-rich country of the black people. This was during the 15th century.

By the early 18th century, a powerful force was underway in midland Ghana — the Ashanti Kingdom. Though it was the biggest kingdom at its height, there were others of almost equal measure in present day Ghana, e.g. Bonnoman, Denkyira, Dagomba, Fante, Akim-Akuapem, Ewe, etc.

Ashanti's quest to expand southwards was met with resistance from the Europeans and also from other indigenous tribes particularly the Fanti people. The ensuing wars were devastating for both Europeans and locals alike. And as powerful and resourceful as Ashanti was, it succumbed eventually to the British, largely due to the latter's sophisticated warfare tactics and weaponry. And with the defeat of Ashanti, the last stronghold of the local resistance against colonization, Ghana's land was lost.

So at what point did the trading missions or posts become political offices through which European monarchs prescribed and proscribed behavior for the black people? Were the trading missions turning up short with profits? Were the trading commodities, be it precious minerals, artefacts or slaves, turning up short with supply? Were traditional authorities demanding fairer deals, as a result of which they had to be rendered politically (or militarily) inept? Were European traders growing deep and insatiable pockets? Or perhaps, it's just the domineering spirit of man?

Historians have done their best to postulate theories and ideas to answer these questions but History itself is a giant fable depending on your perspective and motive. Those who can tell us exactly what happened are dead and gone, we who are here today would do well not to impugn their intentionality. The future is all that matters now.

Defeat of the Ashantis, by the British forces under the command of Col. Sutherland, July 11th 1824

Source: Wikipedia

The political organizations of the various peoples of precolonial Ghana were quite mature. These were mainly monarchical systems with nested organizational structures and cultures. There were urban areas as well as faraway hinterlands. So let it not be said that the white man came and conquered an impoverished uncivilized people. There was civilization, the African civilization, our civilization.

When Fernäo Gomes and his workers arrived in Elmina, it is partially not true that our people did not know of or had not previously interacted with white people and their culture. Through trading routes up North Africa, sub-Saharan peoples had made contact with Europeans, although it is understandable for the vast majority of the people then to plead guilty of this charge, certainly, some of our people had long made contact with the white man and his culture.

During the height of the Ashanti kingdom, Kumasi — the seat of its government, was a developed city by some accounts in that time; from literacy to who knows what it would have become if that gradual organic growth had not been interrupted.

Growing up in the eighties, we heard a lot of stories about how Europeans brought fancy artefacts and other technological implements that awed our forebears. That Schnapps was as valuable as gold. That, ordinary mirrors were bartered for gold and slaves. That guns and ammunitions were exchanged exorbitantly for gold. That a tot of whisky was exchanged for some amount of gold. Whiles these anecdotes may be true, it doesn't mean our people were stupid. We have to remember that scarcity is the driver of the supply and demand process.

Gold was so abundant that it was not as valuable as it is today for the early Ghanaian, the *Gold Coastian.* We were and still, are made of wealth.

Whiles the masses of people lived in mud houses with thatch roofs, urban centers were replete with impressive houses and public buildings. Generally, the evidence shows that people lived well and were cruising in a comfortable trajectory to home-grown development before it was skewed by Europeans. Two notable theories have been postulated to justify or explain this usurpation, i.e. modernization and dependency theories. I would not in this essay stick to academic citation styles. I will try to summarize and paraphrase.

Modernization theory simply put, is that development is serial or progressive. That the developed countries today were once undeveloped and through a serially progressive process nations moved from a pre-modern state to a modern state (or from undeveloped to developed). This theory was very popular and favored by European scholars in the early 20th century. But as the years went on, it lost the gumption to withstand rigorous intellectual probity.

Other scholars postulated a counter-theory and that is, dependency theory, which explains the process of development as a rather exploitative model where fortunes (particularly natural resources and manpower) from poor regions are channeled to rich or advance regions; simply put, the rich get richer and the poor, poorer.

To me, both theories make sense insofar as development processes are concerned but the theory that will never appeal to my acceptation is the theory of imperialism. Europeans systematically exported to us their language, religion, governance, education, etc. - ultimately, their culture and took from us as imports; our gold, timber, oil, manpower, etc. in a disproportionate manner.

Both modernization and dependency theories can be seen as the inherent product of the three drivers of human behavior as I earlier observed — self-preservation, greed and dominion. It was self-preservation that caused Europeans to build their ships and to develop navigational skills, it was greed that caused them to stay after they had arrived in the Atlantic and finally they saw that to continue enjoying the fruits from Eden, they had to have dominion over our lands to perpetuate their selfish and greedy behavior. This is the negative aspect of selfishness and greed that I earlier talked about.

The drastic effect of European mercantilism on our resources is still being felt today. Since the first colonial ship docked, Africa had had the unfortunate fate of being at the receiving end of Europe's insatiable greed. By early 19th century, it had been almost four hundred years during which Europeans swarmed their countries with Africa's manpower in the form of slavery, powering their plantations and industries. Europeans conquered Africa for thing only; they masterminded an exploitation model that suppressed indigenous populations and rewarded our elites to fuel the machinery of the exploitation. Today, the situation is no different.

Before we demonize Europeans, let us consider this. Imagine the situation were reversed and it was a black man who stepped down from the first colonial ship. With the same expertise, technology and weapons the Europeans had. What would we have done with the teeming naïve, primitive and simple white people? Fair play? No. I believe that a human being, in the absence of consequence, would always take advantage of others or the situation.

Now let us look at the other side of the coin, lest we focus too much on all the bad things Europeans did to us. There's a tendency with us to attribute the cause of all our problems to Europeans and what they did to us centuries gone and to romanticize our part of that history. How can we know what African nations would have become had they not been colonized? In modern day Ghana, there was Dagomba, Gonja, Navro, Bonnoman, in the North, Ashanti in midland, Akim and Akuapem in the East, Fanti, Ewe, Ga, etc. along the Atlantic Ocean.

There were trading and other social contacts amongst these nations but there was also antagonism which occasionally resulted in battles. Amongst all these, Ashanti was proving very successful in its expansion, so would Ashanti have conquered all the others and formed one kingdom? Or would we today have twenty different nations on the piece of land called Ghana today?

Would our languages have developed to a point where they would be able to accommodate all the concepts of the advanced world? Would Dagbanli have a term for molecule? Would Yoruba have a terminology for quantum mechanics? Perhaps yes. These questions are vital because Africa would not have been able to live in isolation from the rest of the world which was leapfrogging in development.

Sooner or later, our monarchs would not have been able to withstand dissent in the populace; as people got more education they would have asked for human rights, political rights, economic rights and democracy would have been inevitable. So, would the republic of Ashanti or the various republics, have been able to develop indigenous institutions to meet the demands of modern life?

Ethiopia, the oldest country in sub-Saharan Africa had not been through colonization in its traditional sense. Between 1936 and 1941, it was occupied by Italy but had largely managed to oppugn off European invasions. 1935 Time Magazine's Man of the Year, Haile Selassie l, had sought to modernize Ethiopia with brilliant ideas which yielded some appreciable results. Its timeless indigenous rule until now has still not given us the development Pan-Africanists would hope for. Chronic poverty is still widespread, only 39% adult literacy rate despite its ancient script, human rights are violated, healthcare is miserably inadequate, etc.

Liberia, un-colonized, is another unmistakable example of failure. Freed slaves from America who felt the need to return to Africa and pursue their aspirations came and mixed with the indigenes to form a nation. The former slaves discriminated against their fellow blacks who were indigenous to the area because they were uncivilized in their opinion. This led to sociopolitical and economic exclusion of the locals and later led to the many civil wars that had crippled the nation. Liberia is now making baby-steps towards development but still fraught with the African condition of bad leadership and of course, corruption.

Is this what our collective fate would have been whether or not the Europeans had colonized us? Or are African populations naturally conditioned for failure? It is an interesting thing to note that any country in the world that is black dominated, it doesn't matter where, whether on the continent itself or in the West Indies, majority of the country's population is also poor and in most cases unnecessarily so, because of the abundance of untapped resources.

The evidence suggest that our traditional institutions are not without problems. It was the British that outlawed human sacrifices in *Fantiland* and the rest, it is the same English law that outlawed Female Genital Mutilation (FGM); many examples abound. Today, there are certain traditional chiefdoms which do not have chiefs simply because of disagreement on who to select. The kingmakers cannot agree on which bloodline to select from. Sometimes, the impasse is resolved only after bloodshed.

In Rwanda, without the white man, two African tribes arose against each other to determine which one was better positioned to lead the nation. The result was a havoc similar only to the Black Death itself. In Congo, Nigeria, Ghana, Central African Republic, Sierra Leon, Liberia; in fact, show me one African country that has not seen its share of civil war and destruction thereof? These conflicts were not brought on by Europeans, perhaps not directly, they are the result of failed institutions, both traditional and Victorian.

Before the Europeans, our gold was extracted by artisanal miners with limited skills and technology. Ghana is second to South Africa in terms of gold production in Africa today. In 2011 alone, Ghana produced about 100 tons of gold. I believe this is all due to advanced mining technology which developed from the earlier mining practices introduced by the Europeans. illegal artisanal mining, called locally in Ghana as *Galamsey* and facilitated by our own people, has caused massive destruction of natural resources and is one of the chief inducers of deagrarianization of rural land which would otherwise have contributed to our food supply.

It was the Europeans who introduced new farming methodologies that aimed at increasing cocoa production; number one, two, four and five top cocoa producing countries in the world are Cöte d'Ivoire, Ghana, Nigeria and Cameroon respectively, all along the Atlantic Ocean's Gulf of Guinea. It would not be a mistake to say that it was the European contact that intensified the interest in farming cocoa because they provided the market for it. I grew up in Accra and I don't know of any traditional food uses for cocoa, maybe city life has not given me the privilege.

What about food? *Manihot esculenta* aka Cassava and Maize (sweet corn) were brought from South America to Africa by the same Portuguese ships that carried their guns. Today, not a single Ghanaian can say their stomach has never been warmed by these crops. Even if as an adult your culinary preferences have changed, you were once a baby who sucked milk from your mother's breast which was produced by the efficacy of these crops. An Ashanti dares not play with his *Fufu* and can an Ewe man live without his Eworkple, or an Igbo, his Eba? Certainly not.

Who can measure accurately the damage caused by the food shortage of 1983 in Ghana or Ethiopia? I remember my parents' stories of what they had to do to keep body and soul together. Famine caused tribes of the early people to migrate from place to place in search of arable land that was friendly to their staple food crops, today almost all tribes are comfortably settled due in part to the new crops introduced to us by the same imperialistic European.

The Ghana Statistical Service says Ghana's population was a little over 2 million in 1921 and increased to about 6.7 million in 1960 when the first republic was established. By 1970 it was 8.6 million. It also says that beginning from the early 20th century the population has been steadily increasing. If we are to use a variety of retrogressive statistical analysis, I believe the population size before Europeans arrived would have been much lesser than 1921's 2 million.

In that same report, the GSS says the growth is attributable in part to "declining mortality and constant fertility levels". Is this coincidental? That Ghana's population saw Usain Bolt growth in the same time the Europeans were around?

Well, according to the most authoritative source in this matter, the Ghana Statistical Service, it was because death rates stopped increasing and more people started having more children. Very basic but it suffices.

Before the Europeans, it would have been possible to see a few medical practitioners come occasionally from Cairo to offer their services to wealthy families. It was also possible to see native doctors carry out caesarian section or other surgeries at substantial costs. The broad majority of people relied on native doctors aka herbalists who went around their patients' homes to treat them or built some shacks to accommodate their inpatients.

Patients who were impatient with slow treatments of herbalists or just concerned with their unsuccessful treatment rate might opt for *juju* men to invoke and supplicate to the spirits. I know this because the evidence has not vanished. Today, 2017, there are native doctors and we all know what they do. Neither can we feign ignorance of the so-called prayer camps and *juju* men whose services are sought after.

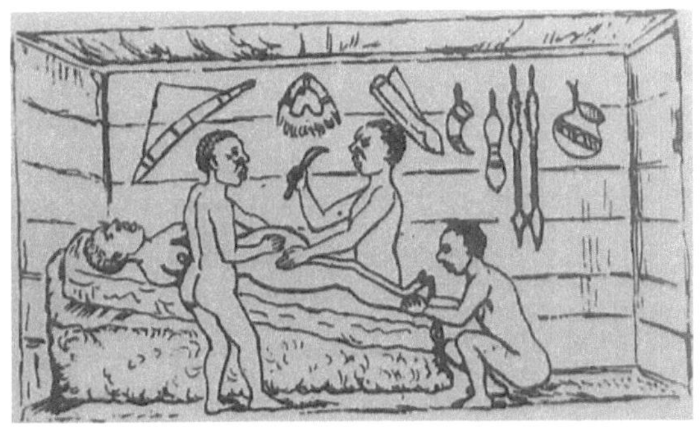

"Successful Cesarean section performed by indigenous healers in Kahura, Uganda. As observed by R. W. Felkin in 1879." Reported in Felkin R. W. "Notes on labour in Central Africa". Edin Med J 1884;29:922-30. as cited in Dunn PM. 'Robert Felkin MD (1853-1926)

Even after all the work the white people have done to bring us quinine, made from a tree bark discovered in South America and chloroquine, a laboratory drug, malaria is still one of the main causes of death in most African countries today — because our governments say there is no money. It is therefore not difficult to imagine that before his arrival, malaria and other ailments had kept our populations stagnant where new babies cancel out the old in tandem.

Some of the sicknesses that are easily treated by a mere visit to the chemist shop today would have meant certain death for the precolonial African. Herbalists, as gifted as they were, would not have been able to provide proper and adequate healthcare, but western education brought new insights and their science based medicine; today our nations can boast of competent doctors who can cut your tummy open, take out your appendix and by a few hours' time, you'd be home swallowing *Banku* again.

Old age and native medicine are not good friends at all. No wonder a lot of reverence was given to people who made it to old age. Today life expectancy for Africans has increased, plus the aged can now reduce body pains and improve general health because of modern medicine.

Poor antenatal practices also had a serious bearing on population growth; stillbirths and sickly children would definitely not impact our population positively. In just a century, from a meager 2 million, Ghana's population is now nearly 30 million. But what does this population spurt mean for our future development? This is a broad topic and certainly cannot be treated lightly in a few paragraphs.

Good healthcare and increases in food production provide the basis for population growth. It would be a fair assumption that primitive healthcare was a hazard that didn't help our populations to grow. Let it be remembered that, it is primitive not because it is African but because it shares characteristics of primitive systems elsewhere. Like those of Britain before the Romans arrived.

Another explanation or argument for the stagnant population in the period before the 1921 census is the Trans-Atlantic Slave Trade. Is it a coincidence that our population started its steady spurt decades after the end of the Atlantic slave trade in the 19th century?

Beginning from the 15th century, millions of Africans were taken as slaves and sent to the New World where they were subjected to unimaginable suffering and the total annihilation of their human rights.

Professor Patrick Manning in his work: Slavery and African Life; Occidental, Oriental, and African Slave Trades, published in September, 1990, estimates that about 12 million slaves were put on ships docked along the Atlantic Ocean. He also estimates that about 1.5 million of these slaves died before they arrived at their various destinations in the Americas. This is exempted from the immeasurable deaths resulting from slave raids on the African continent itself.

The brute force with which slave raiders acquired their merchandise could not have been without massive casualties. Sometimes, whole communities were ambushed and obliterated in a matter of hours. The lucky ones might have been those who perished because they died honorably and exercised the human spirit to resist, at all costs, any infringement on their fundamental rights. Those who were injured beyond reasonable treatment costs would have simply received coup de grâce. In such instances, we can comfortably assume that only a fraction of the members of the community reached their export destinations.

People who support this repugnant phenomenon say that there had long been Intra-African slave trade before the Portuguese docked their ships and that they only took advantage of an existing activity. While this is true, it was not as deleterious to our populations as the Atlantic slave trade.

My father who grew up in the village and adept at my people's oral tradition once told me about how one of the villages called Daalg in the Nabdam district of Ghana came to be and how its villagers have been the subject of friendly mockery by other Nabdam people. According to the story, one of the founding patriarchs of Nabdam bought a slave, a huge and well-built man, probably from Gao slave traders and settled him on that village. In trying to name the area the slave had been settled on, the patriarch could think of no name but Daalg, meaning "the bought". Today descendants of that one slave are in the thousands and have populated an area which otherwise would have been deserted.

Slaves in Africa enjoyed some rights. Their masters were not whip-wielding white capitalists who cared only about profits. Their masters were fellow Africans who understood their situation and treated them with respect. Slaves in Africa were lucky, unlike their counterparts in the Americas whose sweat and blood formed part of the manure that boosted the fortunes of their business-minded masters. Intra-African slave trade cannot be used to justify what happened to our populations.

In the 1970s when archaeologist Peter Shinnie excavated a site in Daboya, Gonjaland in the North of Ghana, he never thought that he would discover facts that would highlight the treachery of slavery. He found that by the early 16th century, there was a burgeoning community of people who made life from their rock salt industry. By 1890, according to the website of the Ghana Museums and Monuments Board (GMMB) under a page entitled "Archaeological Sites and other sites of historical-cultural relevance to Ghana", the whole community, together with their culture was lost to slave raiders.

Where are they? The whole community was collectively lost, it would be fair to assume that at least in some raids, a lot of them were captured at once and sent away. So if they were lost to intra-African slave trade, would it not have been possible for some of their descendants to trace their roots from information they would have gotten through oral tradition passed down by the original slaves?

The descendants of the early Daboyans cannot trace their ancestry because their forebears were sent to the Americas or even Asia where they were scattered and stripped of their identities. Working all day on an empty stomach would not have afforded them the luxury of remembering their homeland; neither could the whipping. Thanks to the bravery and diligence of the abolitionists, descendants of those people now enjoy full rights and comfort as their Caucasian counterparts in the

United States of America. At least, that's some consolation.

Aside the direct impact of slavery on our populations, slavers were interested in certain demographics that affected procreation. Able-bodied young men and women were their main target. So tell me again, how many people were left to fuse spermatozoa and ova to procreate? The level of exploitation of Africa by European slave traders was so huge that after over 400 years, the white men themselves saw that it was too much and not nice and so they stopped. Or was it rather the abolitionists?

There was transfer of spermatozoa, ova and manpower in the Ashanti Kingdom as well as other kingdoms of pre-colonial Africa. In Ashanti, slaves from northern and southern territories formed a substantial proportion of the total manpower that empowered the kingdom. Anecdotal evidence suggests that there was reproduction between enslaved Northern men, known for their height and muscle and Ashanti women because the Ashanti people have been known to be naturally not heighted and they wanted hefty men for war. The resulting children were not bastardised because Ashanti is a matrilineal society.

When our brothers and sisters were chained and loaded onto ships and sent away as slaves, little did we know that their children would be the ones to pioneer the fight for their freedom from slavery and ours from colonialism. W. E. B. Du Bois, Marcus Garvey, Martin Luther King Jr. and Malcolm X are all descendants of slaves taken from Africa to the Americas and due to their hard work and that of many others we are free. Martin Luther King Jr. was shot and killed for doing this. Others also died in the struggle. Others were imprisoned and still, others suffered physical and psychological wounds.

Was our lost through the Atlantic slave trade the price we had to pay for our collective freedom as black people? Especially considering the fact that a locomotive power was inevitably headed for our coasts? I mean the Gulf of Guinea couldn't have hidden itself from the Europeans forever. By 1969 when some

African countries were still reprieving from their independence struggle, the white man had pillaged every corner of Earth and was looking elsewhere — the heavens. In that year Apollo 11's Neil Armstrong, the first man to achieve such a feat, landed on the moon on some kind of prospecting. Earlier in 1957 when Ghana was celebrating independence from the British, the first artificial satellite, Sputnik I was sent into orbit by the Soviet Union.

You can't win all the time, it would be naïve to believe otherwise. The United States of America, the foremost world superpower today, was itself a colony of the British Empire. Huge taxes were exacted by the British monarchs. England, land of the British, at the time of the Roman invasion was just a piece of island with jungle-dwelling people occupying some parts of it. The Roman Empire was also not the pioneer of world dominion.

At various periods there were sometimes simultaneous world systems and power blocs. Considering the proximity of Greece to North Africa and the Middle East where the earliest civilizations began, it was possible that the Greco-Roman civilization was influenced substantially by those earlier ones. And now, Anglo-Saxon cum American civilization, the grandchild of the Greco-Roman civilization has been thrust upon us. Truly, what goes around, comes around.

The western Roman Empire fell in the 5th century. The eastern half of it, the Byzantine Empire lasted a thousand more years. It was also brought to an end by the Ottoman Empire during the conquest of Constantinople in 1453. Greece, land of the founders of the Hellenistic civilization was under the control of foreigners, the Oghuz Turkish who had established the Ottoman Empire. Before long, dissent arose and a feeling of nationalism engulfed the Ottoman Empire leading to the independence of Greece and other Balkan States. The history of world politics is so interesting, sometimes it may serve as a comic relief on a stressful day.

Before the Roman Empire, similar fluctuations and shifts in power occurred. These were mainly centered on powerful individuals who were driven by megalomania and grandeur. In all these conquests, people were killed, slaves were taken, in fact in Rome, slaves were used for amusement in their Colosseum where they fought to death, indigenous peoples were bereft of their lands and were culturally dislodged, the cost and lost cannot be estimated. I am trying here to let you understand the normalcy of what happened to us, Africans.

If you find yourself in Tunisia today, you should not let it escape you to visit Carthage to experience its modern residential milieu. That is today. Almost 2,000 years ago, Scipio Aemillianus, a Roman General torched Carthage to the ground and enslaved the surviving ten per cent of its population of five hundred thousand. Now all those brave Cathaginians who built that flourishing ancient city are gone and buried with them, all that they could've accomplished.

The world has seen many nations but only a few remain today. Most of the nations have been lost to history. During the 2018 World Cup, I saw supporters of

Egypt wearing headdresses that ancient Egyptian pharaohs wore, I presume it was to show the might of the *pharaohic* Egyptian football team but that is quite something, considering that the inhabitants of ancient Egypt were swept under the carpet of history at the hands of its current rulers who now see it fit to share in the glory of their ancient foes.

The quest for dominion over others is the affliction that man had brought from his maker and it seems, it would be the same thing to send him to his maker. The Manhattan Project, borne out of the need to win wars and maintain superior power, had led to the proliferation of nuclear power which in my opinion is one of the rare threats to our civilization.

Now we are free. Europeans have apologized and left our countries for us. Africans have also apologized, especially by traditional authority since it was with their aiding that the slaves and wealth were taken. And yes, no amount of apology can repair and repay the damages and stolen wealth respectively but albeit apologies have been rendered. Acceptance of guilt, and remorse are a powerful combination to fortify us for a brighter future.

We have no choice but to look forward. But looking forward doesn't mean we should look on sheepishly, we have to look forward through the lens of the past and understand how to be free (probably because we've been enslaved for so long we don't know how to assert our freedom). Because you can be free on paper but in practice you're not. This is embodied in one of my favorite quotes "none are more hopelessly enslaved than those who falsely believe they are free" by Johann Wolfgang von Goethe, a very astute man indeed.

AFRICAN UNITY?

Dr. Kwame Nkrumah spent the last twelve or so years of his life in pursuit of an agenda to bring all independent African countries to form a USA lookalike, the United States of Africa. In this, he and his compatriots had hoped that a united African sovereignty would better position us to further the cause of our political and economic freedom.

Although this may be debatable, at face value it sounds laudable and prudent. However laudable, this quest would send some of the founding figures to their early graves and others, loss of power. No wonder the African Union, the product of their efforts has now become a forum for broad discussions with little action; leading some curious minds to question its relevancy and usefulness in the face of all the issues that beset the continent.

Last night, while I was asleep, a mosquito sound woke me up and I was instantly lucid because of the slap I gave myself by my human "fight" instinct to kill the mosquito before it infected me with malaria, which I would have treated easily. What of the many in Africa without health insurance?

After a little tussle with my attempt to go back to sleep, I gave up and decided to use the opportunity to ruminate over some issues regarding Africa but particularly the African Union. After more than 50 years since its founding, can we say confidently that we are cruising in a comfortable trajectory to the dream of a united Africa? Perhaps yes. A lot of strides have indeed been made by the African Union (AU).

But in the early days, its predecessor, the Organization of African Unity (OAU) had not lived up to expectation regarding post-independence internal power-grabbing struggles of its Member States or African countries in general. Some have argued that, the founding goals were too general, creating room for conjecture and lack of specificity.

Applause should therefore go to its leadership, first amongst them, Col. Muammar Gaddafi, who in

1999 passed a resolution to disband the OAU and replace it with the AU which had been touted as structurally different. The new organization, with more focus on gradual economic integration rather than, the hitherto political federation, has resulted in the creation of many economic areas such as the Economic Community of West African States (ECOWAS).

Aside economic integration, the AU's Peace and Security Council has played leading roles in times of conflict throughout the many civil wars that have bedeviled the continent for so long. All 55 countries on continental Africa as well as islandic Africa are members of the AU as of today and mandatorily have representations on the Assembly of the AU which is composed of Heads of State and Governments. With many organs to tackle various focus areas and an elaborate administrative and constitutive architecture, one can say that the AU is structurally robust. The AU's main problem now is the same problem you would hear everywhere you go in Africa — money.

Nevertheless, it has set out on an ambitious undertaking called Agenda 2063, the implementation of which is heavily reliant on its latest brainchild adopted in Kigali in 2016 to impose a 0.2% levy on eligible imports from non-member countries into the AU market. According to the AU, the Agenda 2063 was carefully crafted to solve Africa's problems; mainly human rights, health, peace and security as well as economic prosperity while hoping for political unity.

The Agenda 2063 document has splendid wording and replete with aspirations for the African people. It says it was developed from thorough consultation with a variety of bodies and individuals alike as to the way forward and presents a blueprint for Africa's development in its 50-year scope. But it would not be achievable without money.

The African Union also says that it has been unable to carry out properly its programmes, particularly diplomacy and military functions due to deficits in its budgets. It says the deficits come about because some Member States, averagely thirty countries, fail either in part or in full to render their financial obligations. Other times, its partners, i.e. foreign governments and corporations do not come through with their anticipated gifts (grants, donations, etc.).

In its 2014 financial statement report, almost 50% of its total revenue received of 970 million United States Dollars came from its Partners (foreign). 38% was in-kind or in-service contributions which I believe further interrogation would reveal that a huge chunk of it came from its foreign partners. The African governments themselves, for whose benefits the AU exists contributed 13%. The figure below was designed with data from the AU official report on its finances for the year 2014, previous and subsequent years may not be markedly different

AU STATEMENT OF FINANCIAL PERFORMANCE FOR THE YEAR ENDED 31 DECEMBER 2014	
REVENUE	$ '000
Member States' Assessed Contributions	126,051
Partner Funds Realised	474,770
Voluntary Contributions in Kind/Service	368,656
Other Revenue	700
Total	**970,177**

This is the picture of how the AU was funded in 2014, a year after the launch of its flagship Agenda 2063, the vision of which is "An integrated, prosperous and peaceful Africa, driven by its own citizens and representing a dynamic force in international arena".

Let me ask for your candid opinion; Is this a picture of an African development driven by its own citizens? Again, can this lead us to being a dynamic force in international arena? Let me ice the cake; do you know that the newly built headquarters of the African Union Commission (Secretariat of the AU) in Addis Ababa was designed, funded, built and furnished by the Chinese and gifted to the AU?

Don't be surprise to hear a Nigerian peacekeeping officer remark to his girlfriend in a Calabar beer bar that he prefers UN missions to AU missions. Why? Thousands of AU peacekeepers who have been deployed to Sudan and other conflict zones returned unsatisfied with their participation in AU missions. Issues such as poor equipment, feeding and logistics and underpayment are often their complaints.

The AU which is the driving force behind Africa's development should be the target of blame when we discuss our continental problems. Between 2014 and 2016, the African continent's population would have been brought to the brink of extinction if the West (and now increasingly, the East) had not existed.

The Ebola virus first visited its destruction on Africa in 1976 and claimed over 300 lives in that year alone. Many more deaths occurred in the 1970s. Africa's health apparatus, together with AU programmes, remained unsuccessful to develop a cure until the disease reared up its ugly head again in the 2014-2016 outbreak, the largest ever and claimed 12,000 lives out of the nearly 30,000 confirmed cases.

It was only a matter of time before the disease went continental. Most if not all African governments were unprepared for the outbreak; the structures to manage such a pandemic were simply not available. What would have become of us if American and European health institutions had not intervened? After the 2014-2016 outbreak, as usual, we have gone back to the roost waiting helplessly for the next. But Nollywood would not miss out on this — there's a comedy on the outbreak which receives good patronage.

Are we truly poor or what? The way our governments and institutions bemoan of money calls for many questions. We should ask those questions not because we don't know the answers but because we need to understand the answers well. Since 1995, Transparency International conducts a Corruption Perceptions Index which gauges the level of trust or perception of corruption that citizens have about their public institutions.

In the 2016 version, 44 African countries were studied. 35 of them (80%) fell below the global average score. This is how Transparency International describes its scoring "Over two-thirds of the 176 countries and territories in this year's index fall below the midpoint of our scale of 0 (highly corrupt) to 100 (very clean). The global average score is a paltry 43, indicating endemic corruption in a country's public sector".

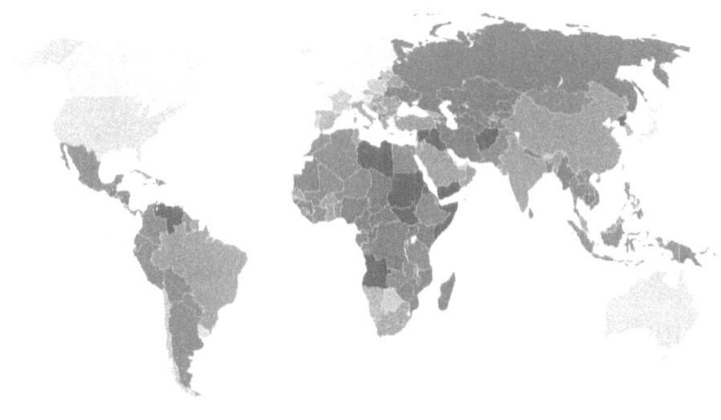

CPI Map, 2016. Source: Transparency International

The above figure is a map showing Corruption Perception Index of 176 countries where yellow means "very clean" and red means "highly corrupt". If you don't squeeze your eyes well you might not notice the yellowish spots on the African continent. If you wear lenses, please don't attempt without them because you will just see one big red dot in the shape of the African continent.

The top 34 countries scoring above 60 were mainly Western countries and a few Asian countries. Only Botswana did Africa the honors by scoring 60, making the 35th position. So according to this report there is endemic corruption in at least 80% of African countries. Although corruption is a global issue, in Africa, I believe the shrewdest of corruption are abundant. In counting the corruption penetration rate of a population, should we look at how widespread it is in a given country? Or Should we focus on the big guns in the leadership who are corrupt? Well, in my opinion, on both accounts Africa would stand tall on a bar chart.

I wanted to include under this section some examples of corruption scandals in Africa and so I googled "biggest corruption scandals Africa", I must have been feeling lucky. In less than half a second, approximately 0.45 seconds, Google returned 545,000 results and so I gave up and returned to write. This does not mean there are 545,000 corruption cases. The actual number could either dwarf or giant this figure. The point being made is to buttress the study by Transparency International that corruption is endemic in Africa. I will tackle the issue of corruption in another chapter.

Can we at this juncture agree that the self-sustainability of the African continent as envisioned by Kwame Nkrumah, Haile Selassie I and later by Col. Muammar Gaddafi cannot be realised under the current configuration? Where at both the micro (national) and macro (continental) levels Africa is dependent on foreign aid. It is almost as if nothing substantial can be done in Africa without our leaders looking first to the West and the East.

In our everyday lives we tend to listen to and obey people who give us food, money and other amenities. A child can misbehave when dealing with strangers but never with its parents otherwise who will feed him or her? How can a person not have the tendency to respect and obey his or her benefactor? In 2011, after having embarked on an airplane to mediate the Libyan crises, the AU envoy was asked by NATO to return which it did obligingly.

Now Col. Muammar Gaddafi, the charismatic figurehead of the AU's restructuring in 1999 has been killed and the AU is still receiving funding in foreign aid.

Recently, China made known an agreement between its government and that of Djibouti to establish a military base on the continent. When the news made the airwaves, it received public backlash. In the final analysis, AU supports the idea. Period.

POVERTY

Poverty is the one true enemy of mankind; the other ills are but its tentacles. And it has had this position for a long time. God Himself says in Deuteronomy 15:11 "For the poor shall never cease out of the land: therefore, I command thee, saying, Thou shalt open thine hand wide unto thy brother, to thy poor, and to thy needy, in thy land." The fear of poverty combined with its inevitability amongst the people of the world is so serious that the Islamic holy book says in al-An'am 6: 151, "Do not kill your children for fear of poverty. We provide for you and for them"

So what amounts to poverty? Should we waste time in defining poverty or should we just mention an example, say, Africa? I think the latter would make matters simple since picture speaks louder than words. Nonetheless, experts have identified that poverty is a broad concept with many dimensions and indicators. Poverty has been discussed under two measurement approaches.

The first is Absolute Poverty which is a basic universal standard required for a human being to survive. We know that without food and water, we cannot live much longer than a few days or weeks. So absolute poverty is the minimum sustenance a Ghanaian, Japanese, Namibian, American or any citizen of any nation requires to keep body and soul together.

This way of measuring poverty can be problematic because a New Yorker, surrounded by the epitome of modern life and wealth would not require the same sustenance as someone in Bangui, assuming both of them are said to be poor by this statistic. Even within the periphery of a nation, say Ghana, if it takes 5 cedis to survive a day in a distant city like Bolgatanga in the North, it would take much more in the capital city, Accra.

Since the early 1990s the World Bank has busied itself setting what it calls global poverty line which was initially set at 1 dollar a day. Since then, the poverty line has been incrementally reviewed every so often to reflect, I assume, declining poverty levels (or inflation) and now stands at 1.90 dollars a day. The poverty line by the way, is the minimum threshold of income needed to sustain life for one person. There's global poverty line (World Bank) and national poverty lines set by

Population living below national poverty line according to the World Bank

	Countries	%	Yr			%	Yr			%	Yr
1	Equatorial Guinea	76.80	2006	21	Gambia, The	48.40	2010	39	Namibia	28.70	2009
2	Madagascar	75.30	2010	22	Senegal	46.70	2011	40	Tanzania	28.20	2012
3	Zimbabwe	72.30	2011	23	Chad	46.70	2011	41	Cape Verde	26.60	2007
4	Congo, Democratic Republic of the	71.30	2006	24	Burkina Faso	46.70	2009	42	Egypt	25.20	2011
5	Guinea-Bissau	69.30	2010	25	Sudan	46.50	2009	43	Uganda	24.50	2009
6	Eritrea	69.00	1993	26	Congo, Republic of the	46.50	2011	44	Ghana	24.20	2012
7	Burundi	66.90	2006	27	Kenya	45.90	2005	45	South Africa	23.00	200
8	Liberia	63.80	2007	28	Rwanda	44.90	2011	46	Algeria	22.60	199
9	Swaziland	63.00	2009	29	Comoros	44.80	2004	47	Botswana	19.30	200
10	Central African Republic	62.00	2008	30	Mali	43.60	2010	48	Tunisia	15.50	201
11	São Tomé and Principe	61.70	2009	31	Côte d'Ivoire	42.70	2008	49	Thailand	13.20	201
12	Niger	59.50	2007	32	Mauritania	42.00	2008	50	Indonesia	12.50	201
13	Zambia	59.30	2006	33	Cameroon	39.90	2007	51	Morocco	9.00	200
14	Togo	58.70	2011	34	Ethiopia	38.90	2005		Africa	44.80	200
15	Lesotho	56.60	2003	35	Angola	36.80	2008				
16	Guinea	55.20	2012	36	Benin	36.20	2011				
17	Mozambique	54.70	2009	37	Nigeria	33.00	2013				
18	Sierra Leone	52.90	2011	38	Gabon	32.70	2005				
19	Malawi	50.70	2010								
20	South Sudan	50.60	2009								

respective countries.

The table below depicts 49 African countries and percentage of their populations living below their respective national poverty line (NPL). The first twenty countries must be home to direct descendants of Lazarus the Beggar, from 76.80% to 50% of their populations live in poverty according to the World Bank.

DR Congo, with a population of 82 million is seen in the table with 71.30% and yet some estimates say that the Congo has 70% of the world's coltan, one-third of the world's cobalt, more than 30% of its diamond reserves, and one-tenth of its copper. Sitting on all this wealth by an extremely poor people should interest social scientists for further study and analysis.

But we those who are on the ground should know better than solely rely on the World Bank's estimates. The current global poverty line (the lower) of 1.90 dollars would be 8.36 cedis in Ghana per day, 58.52 cedis per week and 234.08 cedis per month (at the time of writing). But these were not the figures used to arrive at Ghana's poverty penetration of 24.2% as seen in the table above.

Ghana uses two figures to set its national poverty line, a lower (792 GHS/year) and an upper (1,314 GHS/year) per adult (meaning child poverty is excluded) to calculate its national poverty levels. This translates into 2.22 GHS/day and 3.70 GHS/day or $0.49/day and $0.82/day respectively.

World Bank also uses two figures, i.e. \$1.90 and \$3.10 as the global standards to measure poverty levels. \$1.90 being the stricter statistic below which a person is extremely poor. People who live on above \$1.90 and below \$3.10 are better off but still poor. For me, poverty is poverty, the two-tier approach to measuring poverty lines is a matter of policy convenience.

The thing is such that the lower the standard (poverty line), the lower the poverty penetration rate to be measured. Got it? How convenient therefore that the nation of Ghana would adopt in 2013, figures that ensure that it meets the first MDG target of reducing poverty by 50% by 2015. The actual poverty is much worse than 24.2% arrived at by using the national standards because \$0.49 or \$0.82 a day must be referring to the poorest of the poor. A decent loaf of bread in Ghana would cost no less than 5 cedis or \$1.11 (at the time of writing).

In Greater Accra region which hosts the capital city and which according to the national standard is the region of the country with the lowest incidence of poverty, one would require a minimum of 5 cedis to cook the poorest meal — I mean gari and sardine.

Secondly, the headcount is only on adults meaning that their children who should automatically suffer child-poverty are not included in the 24.2% poverty rate of Ghana. Ultimately, it also means that it is not 24.2% of the total population that is poor but 24.2% of a section of the population — adults. We also know that poor people have large family sizes, meaning that a huge chunk of the child population is living in poverty de facto.

The point being made is that when the national poverty line which is set by individual nations is too low, it excludes a lot of people who by all accounts of poverty are poor. If you live in Accra or any major city and earn between 200 and 300 cedis, not counting jobless people, you would not be considered poor by this headcount. But the actual people who earn this amount know that they are poor.

On average, it means that you'd have 8.33 cedis or $1.85 to depend on each day. But in the cities this income cannot ensure that you have time to think about your children's education, you cannot hope for well-balanced meals and neither can you pursue other aspirations of the human spirit. But your government says you are not poor.

Being Ghanaian, it should be understandable that I would choose Ghana to illustrate my points. But the Ghanaian story is not only for Ghana; it is for Africa. This is how poverty is being measured across the length and breadth of SSA, against which policy is made to eradicate it. Any wonder then, that poverty reduction efforts in Africa have been largely futile? In computer terminology, there's a concept called GIGO (garbage in garbage out), when you feed policymaking with garbage data, you'd get garbage results.

Converging consensus amongst researchers and scholars alike is that the country of Ghana, like many African countries, is growing in terms of GDP and other indicators but nonetheless, poverty is rife. What is so different about us, Africans, that all the stringent and honest efforts by our governments to extricate us from poverty have failed? Someone would have me phrase the preceding question as "what is so wrong with African governments that their poor peoples' stringent and honest efforts to develop themselves have failed. Which is which?

There is a certain village in Ghana, where for a whole week nobody in that village sees money with their naked eyes, I mean money, including coins. They live on harvested crops from their subsistence farming. There are other villages where only privileged people feel the crispiness of a ten-cedi note occasionally. There are many of such villages in every sub-Saharan African nation which are so far removed from civilization that the village chief drinks 'pure water' only on a big festival day.

For these villages and their inhabitants, untreated bacteria-infested water is the norm, healthcare is crude and it is easier for a camel to pass through the eye of the needle than for their children to get good education. Though they may fill their stomachs with their farm produce and shelter themselves, on other accounts of poverty, they are positively poor.

It says Ghana has 24.2% poverty rate according to the World Bank and yet this is what the then flagbearer of NPP and now president of the Republic of Ghana, Nana Akufo-Addo had to say during the 2016 general election "Today the greatest challenge confronting our nation is the unprecedented high level of unemployment among the youth. According to the World Bank about 48% of Ghanaians between the ages of 15-24 years are unemployed whiles over 18% of those aged between 25-64 years are inactive or unemployed and actively looking for jobs. More than 150,000 students leave school at various levels of education every year for the job market in Ghana".

Though this is not meant to equate poverty with unemployment or vice versa, it certainly helps to understand the latitude of poverty in Ghana. I shudder to imagine the actual situation for countries comprising the first 20 on the list in the table above.

The other approach of measuring poverty is Relative Poverty which is defined in relation to the economic conditions of other members of the society in question. So poor people would be identified in Lagos not by a global statistic but by those people's comparative standing with the economic status of other Lagosians. Same with Pelungu, a village in the Nabdam district of Ghana. If a person has lived all his life in Pelungu and is happy to do so, to measure this person's poverty standing, we compare him or her to other villagers in Pelungu and not to the national or international statistics. But what if the whole society is poor by the universal standard?

Both absolute poverty and relative poverty underscore social inequality. That is, members of a given population differ; while some have opportunities, others do not. While some receive social services such as quality healthcare and education; while some eat well-balanced meals at pleasure; while some have jobs; while some have economic rights; while some have sociopolitical rights and so on; others do not.

Poverty comes in degrees both in its manifestation and its causation. Some people are so poor that the sight of food alone is enough to raise their blood pressure; others are malnourished and underfed. Safe drinking water, good sanitation and shelter may be luxurious for some poor people. Such extreme poverty has been the bane of sub-Saharan Africa and similar regions in the world.

The poverty reduction statistics suggesting that it is on the decline create confusion as to their validity because of the emboldened visibility of poverty in sub-Saharan Africa.

From Cape Town to Cairo, all the major cities that by these statistics are lowest in their respective countries in terms of poverty prevalence are also home to the dreary scars of extreme poverty. Nested in these cities are shanty towns larger both in terms of size and population than the country of Monaco. The entrance greeting on these towns is one word written in caps — POVERTY

Again, in Accra, 2.5 cedis is the regular price for a one-litre bottled water from a certain bottling company but there are hotels, restaurants and other social places where the same bottle of water is sold for higher amounts up to 20 cedis. The consumer has to now choose where to buy from depending on their buying power. Perhaps these examples do not speak much by themselves because of their invariability across the world but in Africa the huge gap between them speaks volumes and especially reflects the level of social inequality on the ground.

Whiles in the past laws were used to enforce segregation, pricing is used today. Poor people have their own schools, hospitals, social centres not because the others have explicit laws barring their admittance but because of affordability.

Over the years SSA has received support in all forms to eradicate poverty aside its own internally generated funds. Economic growth in terms of GDP is rising meagerly but for reasons peculiar to Africa, the growth has not been met with commensurate reduction in poverty. In 1990, the percentage of sub-Saharan Africans living below the poverty line was 54% (or 276 million), in that same year it was 45% (505 million) for South Asia, also a developing region. While in 2013 the South Asian poverty level had reduced to 15.1%, sub-Saharan Africa is still lazily perambulating in the 40s, in fact 113 million more people have sunk below the poverty line. See table below.

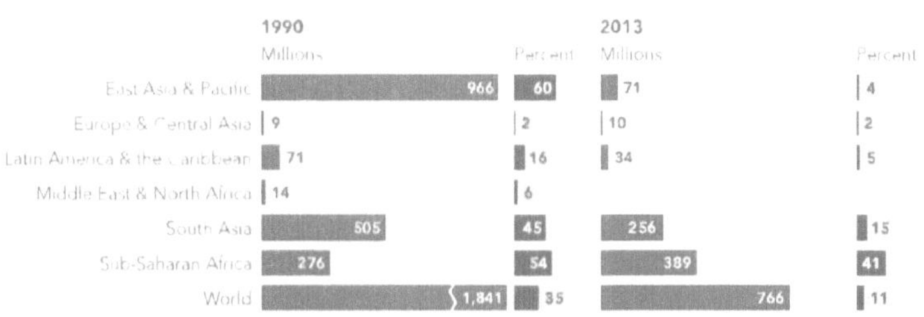

Number and share of population living on less than $1.90 a day (2011 purchasing power parity or PPP) (%), 1990 and 2013

Latin America and the Caribbean is another region with consolatory story. Between 2000 and 2014, the headcount of people living below its poverty line of $4 dropped from 45% of its population to 25% while those living below its stricter lower poverty line of $2.5 a day dropped from 28% to 14%. Such remarkable results have been attributed to growth in the overall economy as well as other policy measures, chief amongst them is a bunch of programmes collectively called Conditional Cash Transfers

(CCTs). This trend, if continued could see the eradication of chronic poverty in the region in a couple of decades or less.

East Asia & Pacific regional poverty reduction is yet another success story. The region is home to emerging superpower China with a population of 1.37 billion as at 2015, more than 300 million more people than the entire population of Africa. As at 2013, China's poverty rate fell to 1.9% of its population. The entire East Asia and Pacific region reduced extreme poverty from 60% (almost a billion) in 1990 to 4% (71 million) in 2013.

While poverty reduction efforts in the three regions discussed; South Asia, Latin America & the Caribbean and East Asia & Pacific are yielding dividends, they are not without problems but certainly promising. Africa's ominous poverty trend is a cause for concern not just for the poor in Africa but for the rich as well.

What are we not getting right in Africa? Is something wrong with our constitutive make-up as black people? Are our governments simply hamstrung in a gigantic global economic space where the sharks eat up the salmons? Is it a case of lack of expertise in governance? Is it a case of lack of sincerity in leadership's commitment to solving the problems? Is policy short-circuiting somewhere? I would not invite physiological burden on my person by trying to answer these questions. Ignorance is bliss, but still I find that corruption underpins everything in Africa.

Education is a key instrument for reducing poverty which is why the Africa Union's New Partnership for African Development (NEPAD) selected 10 African countries in 2005 to implement a school feeding programme. The purpose was to encourage school attendance at the basic levels because often children from poor backgrounds are more wont to truancy.

In Ghana, the programme progressed successfully in its first few years, but later when one of its partners, the Netherlands, commissioned an audit of the programme by PricewaterhouseCoopers, it found that the programme had been fraught with “widespread corruption". Mainly the issues were poor procurement practices, disappearance of programme funds, use of cheap and unwholesome ingredients, etc. This is what I meant when I said earlier that corruption underpins everything - even money meant for the feeding of poor pupils. I have a firm believe that Africa's poverty is not as a result of lack of resources but as a result of the poor use of them.

EDUCATION

Guinness book of world records needs no introduction. According to the Guinness book, the oldest university in the world is the University of Karueein in Fez, Morocco which was founded in 859 AD. The next oldest would be Egypt's Al-Azhar University also founded in the first millennium, precisely in 975 AD. These were decades before the oldest university in England, Oxford was conceived.

In sub-Saharan Africa, we can talk about Timbuktu. At its height it served as home to many learning centres. Widespread or inclusive education was not until the Europeans arrived and since then its importance and pursuit has never known decline. But the point remains that Africans had been used to the concept of intellectual development long before Europeans came.

With the arrival of the Europeans came the missionaries with their schools and new languages for doing business. The Whiteman had thoroughly convinced us that their culture and expertise were the route to follow. Soon, the herdsmen, farmers, artisans etc. reduced in number to embrace formal education because success in the future the white people promised was all based on one's ability to speak their language and understand their concepts.

Now we are in the future their civilization promised; of democracy, literacy, knowledge acquisition, science and technology, new methods of sustenance, etc. and a gigantic global village where everything more or less depends on a person's education. The future of the current dispensation is even more so.

Since the dawn of western education in Africa, minority groups including women and marginalized societies have been shortchanged. Women hadn't had the luxury of education for a long time in Africa and now that the situation has changed, the education infrastructure is inundated and sloppy.

Generally, education in developing regions across the world remains unsatisfactory but in Africa, particularly sub-Saharan Africa, it is woefully inadequate and inaccessible at the basic level. Pre-school or kindergarten education should be out of this discussion because it is not the preserve of the poor. Secondary and tertiary education are cousins of basic education in this context — abysmal.

The general consensus is that education leads to better living conditions and hence the eradication of poverty, there's no doubt therefore that it is one of the important items on the plate of policymakers in African countries.

The degree of poor education on the African continent is more profound at the basic level. Individuals below the age of 14 years represent a significant proportion of the national populations of African countries ranging from 35% to 40% of their respective national populations. Per national aspirations and international treaties, all these children must be in school, the broad majority of whom rely on public schools, i.e. government run schools.

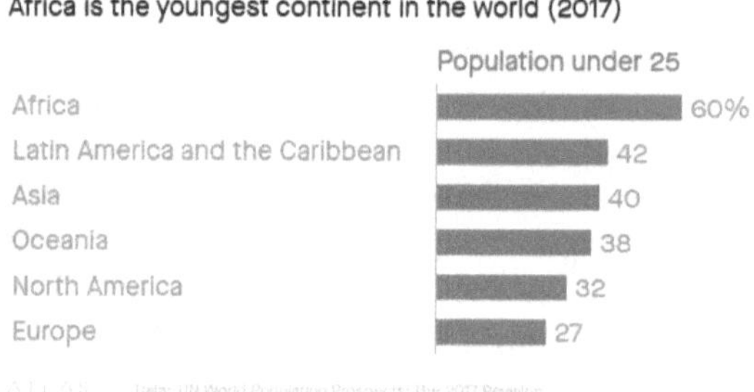

This is, no doubt, a serious burden for African governments. Fifty years ago this burden perhaps would have been halved because parents were not so enthused by girl-child education and others, being conservative in favor of the old world preferred their boys on the farm or herding. Today, the importance of education is acknowledged even by the unlettered and the burden is hundred per cent strong.

So how are African governments carrying or managing this heavy load? The problem is two-fold; firstly, access and secondly, quality. African governments score abysmally on both fronts. I find that in most African nations, more focus is given to access — creating the opportunity for children to be enrolled in school, what happens after is their fate. Efforts to enhance quality have presumably been hampered by the lack of resources.

Access to education means the physical infrastructure, availability of learning materials and teachers and to some extent, how children commute to school every day. Since the importance of education is well understood, we can reasonably assume that there is policy provision to ensure universal basic education for all.

Sub-Saharan Africa leads the world in terms of percentage of government expenditure on education with an average of 16.79% for the period 2000-2014. This trend underscores the premium governments across SSA are placing on education. Make no mistake, 16.79% in this context does not give SSA a commensurate lead in the world in terms of absolute figures because SSA has a much lower government expenditure, occasioned by its lower GDP.

Some African countries are more effortful and successful than others. For example, Ghana's average for the same period above is 23.83%, South Africa's is 19%

and Zambia's is 7.7%. Despite all these efforts, the UN's Sustainable Development secretariat estimates that 59 million children of school going age are not in school. I want to believe that something wrong happens between the point funds are earmarked for education and the point when those funds actually end up in education. What is that thing?

Across Africa, there are thousands of the so-called open-air schools which are mostly seen in interior areas. They are hilariously nicknamed 'schools under trees' in Ghana. Classes can be held on sunny days but not on rainy days. Class sessions are brought to abrupt end when the weather shows signs of rainfall which often is preceded with heavy winds that scatter books and pupils alike.

In 2011, the Ghana Education ministry estimated about 5,000 schools under trees across the nation. Namibia's education service also estimated in 2013, three hundred and fifty open-air classrooms. All sub-Saharan African countries have their figures.

However, let us not confuse the early 20th century open-air schools of Europe, borne out of a movement to design classrooms with maximum ventilation to reduce the spread of tuberculosis, with the 21st century open-air schools of Africa. Ours is because our governments say there is no money to build proper school buildings.

The average class size number between 35 and 60 pupils, do the math for Ghana's 5000 schools under trees, do same for the rest and you'd realize how many children's future is in jeopardy. The ripple effect of such poor beginning, in later years of education is quite serious. But these are the lucky ones, millions more cannot go to school at all for various reasons but supremely due to poverty.

Your first day in a government school in Africa is the beginning of a long, narrow and uncertain journey with two possible outcomes; failure and pass. Failure here refers to dropping out at some point either by your teacher's assessment or by your own. Pass here does not refer to having attained quality education, it simply means, you have gone through the system.

The learning materials that are given to pupils in class one or grade one or whatever it may be called are the same ones their fathers were given. Their teachers were trained with the same teaching methods as the ones before. Textbooks, writing books, pens and pencils, even chalks for teachers to write on chalkboards are all not in good supply.

Some pupils walk barefooted for kilometers before they get to school, by the time classes begin the little breakfast they ate at home has vanished from their stomachs. The absence of food in the belly causes physiological disparities that make learning a hoax. While their counterparts in Europe are now required to learn how to program computers. Certainly these two dichotomous people have divergent destinations. While the latter can hope to become a nuclear scientist, the former cannot. The poor African child today cannot dare to hope to become; merely to go through the system and hope for the next meal.

In the center of education are teachers and that is also an issue. The problem with teachers is three-fold; availability, motivation and capacity. Government does not have enough teachers to cater for even the poor intake at the basic level; school authorities have been compelled to manage a highly economized timetable where a handful of teachers are spread to cover so many subjects a day. The use of untrained teachers to supplement teaching is also practiced.

Teachers are also underpaid and sometimes salaries are delayed for several weeks or months. This has forced some teachers to improvise by seeking alternative income sources which diffuse their motivation and dedication to their actual charges. In my basic school days, teachers sold snacks during class hours, in my secondary school days, teachers owned farms on school land and recalcitrant students were made to work on these farms and in the universities, lecturers insist students should buy their handouts.

In Ghana and most SSA countries, there's free basic education for all which by all account is laudable. But some teachers being less enchanted, only teach half the material during official class hours and the other half in their so-called extra-classes where pupils are made to pay per session. Failure to attend extra-classes is punishable either by whip or by academic scores.

Capacity building for teachers is another matter. This combined with obsolescence of learning materials, i.e. textbooks, are a dangerous recipe for producing students with outdated knowledge. Some teachers have been administering the same textbook for years, they've become mullahs who can recite the textbook from cover to cover. NASA may have discovered more planets but to these teachers and their students, there are still nine planets. How can we hope for the next astronaut from such humble beginning?

Teachers who take their destinies into their own hands would acquire more education in hopes of getting promoted on the pay scheme but corruption in the management of promotions or deliberate delays as a result of financial constraints make such endeavors less rewarding. Leaving many teachers to graciously embrace the old saying that the teaching profession is not meant for wealth acquisition. Which further exacerbates their disenchantment to giving off their best.

Every year millions of children across Africa are enrolled into basic schools but by the time they reach tertiary level, majority of their cohorts have abandoned school. This pyramidal trend is worrying for many reasons and still the few who make it to tertiary schools leave school for non-existent jobs. International Labour Organisation (ILO) estimates that 50% of the about 10 million yearly graduates from SSA tertiary institutions do not get jobs. If the situation wasn't so dire, how come there's a certain Unemployed Graduates Association of Ghana (UGAG)?

There have long been calls for our education system to be revamped to be industry-friendly so that graduates would leave school with entrepreneurial or job-ready skills. But the curriculums remain the same after all these years. It's as if we know what to do but cannot agree on how to do it. The mass production of graduates without recourse to their employability gives credence to the accusation of ineptitude on the part of our education policymakers.

Our governments are so intent on expanding our economies by attracting foreign direct investments but the foreign companies often bemoan the lack of qualified workforce on the domestic job market. Recently, Aliko Dangote, Africa's illustrious son and the very evidence that the black man is capable, made known a new enterprise in Nigeria but that it will largely be powered by some 30,000 foreign workers. What should Emeka, the jobless graduate from University of Lagos, do?

The same issue of lack of money has caused most public universities to focus on the Humanities and Social Sciences. Even so, large amount of the research upon which teaching is based were conducted by European and American scholars. Recently and occasionally in Ghana, lecturers go on strikes because government has not paid their book and research allowance. Like I said before, the Ghanaian story is not only for Ghana but for the whole of sub-Saharan Africa.

The picture is not all grimly, Africa's burgeoning intelligentsia reflects to a larger extent, individual enterprise in the pursuit of education; despite the huge infrastructural constraints. The 'city youth' of Africa are embracing new channels of education, brought on by digital systems and are leapfrogging into the very belly of the internet to get education. But the 'village youth' of Africa are constantly having to grapple with all the challenges of our dilapidated education service.

I recently visited Achiase, a town in the Eastern Region of Ghana, known for its mammoth flora and natural beauty. It is a few kilometers from Oda which is an old city and has profited from decades of timber trade. Folks there seemed to be quite content with life there; with a myriad of age-long trading in timber, agriculture, fishing, etc. and newer vocational activities in dressmaking, hairstyling, bakery, etc. While I engaged some of the people I met there, I got a sense of nonchalance on their part about migrating to Accra since everything they want is more or less readily available.

My co-traveller and I spent the weekend in a small guesthouse in Osoroase, an adjoining village to Achiase. On the morning of Sunday while I was stretching my legs taking a stroll along its serene and greenish paths amidst dew and bird songs, I saw a field up ahead where kids were playing football. Just young boys, about fifteen of them, properly dressed in football gear. I hastened my steps and was on time to witness a goal. I made the acquaintance of an eleven-year-old Kwabena, a substitute player waiting anxiously for his turn on the pitch.

During my conversation with Kwabena, I learned from him that, not only were they warming up to go to church later that morning, but all of them on the field are pupils of the community school, and were also physically preparing for school the following morning. His English proficiency was good enough and his eyes beamed with hope and excitement for the future. My experience with Kwabena however contrasted so much with what I had learned from the previous day when I met three young girls averagely 16 years old in Achiase.

The first girl stopped school when she entered Junior High School on advice from older neighbors, to learn a vocation. She is now an apprentice baker, hoping to pass out in a couple of years to start her own bakery business. The second girl stopped earlier in class five and also hopes to be a "big hairdresser" she said. The third girl was in the process of stopping school too because most of her friends had stopped and were acquiring skills for immediate employment while she had still not fully grasped the import of going to school.

I got the sense that the cessation of their schooling isn't as a result of poverty because they are spending a lot more money on the vocational training than in the government schools. It is a clear case of choice, the decision of which is marred in the lack of understanding of formal education and its benefits. The third girl for instance did not understand why she would be learning complex mathematical equations while her friends were constantly talking about moneymaking in two years' time.

While the argument can be made that these girls have taken a constructive alternative to formal education, I still fear for their future. I fear that they would soon become teenage mothers, because Achiase as opposed to the serenity of Osoroase is fraught with all the ills of urban life.

It is not only in distant towns like Achiase would you find such interesting polarized interests in education.

The other day, a childhood friend of mine visited and we had a nice time talking about life. I started school with him but after secondary school, things didn't pan out well and he is convinced, formal education is no longer on his agenda.

I wanted to know more. Why? We sat in the same classrooms for nine years and listened to the same teachers so what happened? He told me, all the while we were in school, he didn't understand it all. As a child, he felt he was being compelled to do something he didn't want to do. His father only examined him once out of the 365 days in a year. He said until secondary school, the reason to go to school was very hazy for him. Is my friend making up an excuse to justify his poor academic scores in school? Perhaps, but it is profound in understanding some of the issues in our education system.

So while the onus lies with governments across SSA to provide the basis for education, the decision to be educated lies squarely with the people themselves. Some parents, perhaps as a result of their own lack of education, do not take active interest and participation in the education of their wards. It is said, you can force a horse to the riverbank but you cannot force it to drink.

Back in my primary school days, it was not until I cried on my parents one day that my father delegated my older sister to attend a Parents and Teachers Association (PTA) meeting. It wasn't just me, from class one to class six the student population was about 720 but during PTA meetings, you would not count more than fifty parents. Certainly the awareness for parents to understand their role in the education of their children ought to increase.

HEALTH

Quality of life is essentially health of the people. I will attempt to define Health. It is the maintenance of the body on the basis of longevity.

Long, long before angel Gabriel appeared to Mary which later resulted in the birth of Jesus Christ, Hippocrates was born in Kos, Greece around 460 B.C. It is to his erudition that science based medicine today owes its origin, according to some accounts. He is considered the 'father of medicine' by a lot of well-respected medical concerns and historians alike.

His tenacity for knowledge, especially of science, and his humanist approach to the practice of medicine spurred the process that ousted superstition and religion in the field of professional medicine. The fruits of his diligence and that of many others are now enjoyed by all and sundry across the world, including Africa.

But it all started in Africa, many centuries before Hippocrates was born. The accounts that place on Hippocrates the title of "father of medicine" fail to mention that he studied at the temple of Amenhotep, Egypt. While there, he and many more Greeks, were put through rigorous medical training which they later exported across the Hellenistic world. The students then, would have been reading a bunch of scripts including Papyrus Ebers, part of which details the ingredients for treating headache as "inner-of-onion, fruit-of-the-am-tree, natron, setseft-seeds, bone-of-the-sword-fish, cooked, redfish, cooked, skull-of-crayfish, cooked, honey, and abra-ointment." Bryan, Cyril (1932) The Ebers Papyrus.

Perhaps, they exported the raw material. Later, scholars and practitioners refined and set the tone for proper scientific methodology to diagnosis, treatment and prognosis.

But that was in the olden days. Today, nobody should be interested in monopolizing knowledge, least of all, medicine. It is readily and even sometimes, freely available. Meaning that, what they teach in Oxford, Queen's College in the field of medicine can also be taught at the University of Liberia and both doctors will deliver the same services.

I would not want to talk much about the quality of medical training content in SS Africa but rather the numbers. Because when push comes to shove, any doctor is good enough. Of course this is not meant to diminish the coveted expertise of our doctors. So what do the numbers speak in terms of available modern-day Hippocrates in SS Africa?

The map below shows the various countries in the world and their representations as to their "density of physicians" aka doctor-patient ratio from the latest data available to the World Health Organisation (WHO). In other words, how many doctors are available for 1,000 people within a particular country. Here green means good and yellow means bad. If you didn't know what SS Africa looks like on a map, just look out for the portion with the largest concentration of yellow.

Density of physicians (total number per 1000 population, latest available year)

Doctors are the cornerstone of healthcare. If a country spends millions on building an 'ultra-modern' health facility and still has to rely on specialists from abroad, it may not be said to be taking the matter of healthcare seriously. Similarly, if the only doctors respected in a country are those who acquired their tutelage from abroad then that country cannot boast much.

During the immediate period before the start of the 21st century, it was quite fashionable for parents in SSA to encourage their children to study medicine because it would enable them to travel abroad, especially to Europe and America for greener pasture. Even today, the mentality and motivation to do so have not dissipated.

Due to lack of proper training systems, some governments in SSA have had various arrangements with foreign schools to increase the number of capable physicians at substantial costs. When the selected students go, after having been exposed to better systems elsewhere, some of them do not return. Those who return, not all can stand the test of time for obvious reasons, so they ran back to Europe. Leaving the enormous patients in the hands of very few doctors who swim against the tide to stay and serve; at the scorn of patients.

It is not only doctors who are lured by the beauty of the West, nurses and other health professionals would not reject the offer. This in no way is meant to suggest that there aren't dedicated and selfless people who would choose to stay. Those people exist but rarely; such that an eagle flying over the continent will count them with one eye closed.

I am merely narrating what I have seen. I cannot tell how to increase the number of doctors or how to motivate them to stay. A lot of research reports have answered these questions already. But do we need a scientist to tell us how? The Bible says in Ecclesiastes 10:19 KJV ".... money answereth all things".

Even if the doctors were abundant, where and how would they work? What is the state of distribution of healthcare systems or facilities? Africa is broad and heavily populated. The statistical projections show acute increasing trends. The status quo is already overwhelming. Simply, the physical systems required by doctors are limited. When there are hospitals, doctors complain of specialist equipment, when there is equipment they complain of experts. At every turn, there is a cause for concern, especially for the patient.

Nothing endangers a patient's condition more than fake drugs. These are flooding into our medical stores through distribution channels that often inundate our governments' systems to prevent them. Fake drugs combined with shortage of medical supplies is truly moot and hopeless for providing proper healthcare for the people. Hospitals should be places of reprieve and not places where the danger looms to worsen patients' conditions, to death.

Should it be a crime to be sick in Africa, the punishment of which includes death? The World Health Organisation (WHO) categorizes causes of death into three broad spectrums. Group one comprise "communicable, maternal, perinatal and nutritional conditions", group two are non-communicable diseases and the third are those resulting from injury. The WHO Africa region is bedeviled with group one, which is also described as preventable causes of death.

In 2015, the data shows that 9.2 million Africans died of all three causes. 56.4% of that resulted from preventable causes of death chiefly lower respiratory infections, HIV/AIDS, diarrheal diseases, tuberculosis and malaria, in the order of significance. Five-point-two million people could have lived if the proper preventive measures were in place, that's what it simply means.

Out of the foregoing, 232,000 lives were whisked away by the hand of death due to nutritional deficiencies in 2015. Protein-energy malnutrition and iron-deficiency anemia were the main inducers in this regard. When Hippocrates said there are some diseases that can only be treated by nutrition, he meant well and this should have served some comfort to the poor in Africa but let's postpone that because nutrition is still very expensive.

I am not discussing this because I don't expect people to die. Death is a constant all creatures have. But when more than half of the people dying, many of whom being children under five years, is as a result of preventable causes, we ought to pause for a minute and whip some sense into ourselves.

47% of the 5.2 million cases of preventable causes of death in 2015 were children under the age of five years. In 2010, it was 49% of that year's 5.6 million. In 2005, 50% were children under the age of five of that year's 6.6 million cases and in 2000, it was 56% of its 6.8 million cases. In four years, i.e. 2000, 2005, 2010 and 2015, 12.3

million children under the age of five died of preventable causes of death.

In 2015 for instance, out of the 2.4 million children under five who died as a result of preventable causes of death, 98% were caused by neonatal conditions, lower respiratory infections, malaria, African Trypanosomiasis and diarrheal diseases, according to the WHO data. Newborns and children under five continue to be the most vulnerable population exposed to preventable causes of death in the WHO Africa region.

There's good news. The fight against HIV/AIDS is bearing fruits. In 2010 about 1 million deaths occurred but decreased by 24% to 760,000 in 2015 and it seems the trend is going down. Increased availability of antiretroviral drugs which lame the replication effort of the virus is part of the solution. This should serve some solace considering the fact that about 1.5 million deaths occurred in 2005 from HIV/AIDS in Africa alone.

Available data show that by the year 2000, malaria was 4th -echelon cause of death in Africa claiming 790,000 lives in that year, after fifteen years, in 2015 deaths resulting from malaria have almost halved down to 403,000. Perhaps, another fifteen years is all we need to put the menace behind us.

Diarrheal diseases such as cholera is also reducing according to the World Health Organization. In 2000, it claimed 900,000 lives. In 2015 it took 643,000 lives. Other preventable causes of death in SSA are also seeing a decline but are being replaced by 'lifestyle diseases' such as stroke, heart attacks, etc.

For instance, in 2000, number 4 and 5 causes of death were malaria and measles respectively with a combined havoc of 1.27 million deaths. Fifteen years on, malaria was pushed to the 7th position whiles measles sunk much further down the ranking.

The 4th and 5th positions are now occupied by stroke and ischemic heart diseases (heart attacks) which obliterated 891,000 lives - representing 5.94% of the global cases of the two in 2015. The WHO Africa region recorded the least deaths resulting from the so-called lifestyle diseases, obviously because 'lifestyle' here reflects wealth of the people and not many are wealthy in SSA.

However, let it be remembered that, data collection does not achieve hundred percent coverage of its target group, at least not in this context. Coverage rate would be specially impeded in Africa because of limited systems and cultural issues. Who bothers in an African village to report to the officials the gentle death of a malaria patient at home? Next thing, the flute players gather to whistle out some dirges and the government is non-the-wiser.

The increasing trend in lifestyle-induced causes of death is quite worrying and perplexing at the same time. Worrying because the gains we are making in reducing preventable diseases are being reversed. Perplexing because, how can a rich man's disease affect a poor man? What lifestyle are the people of Africa adopting as a result of which their longevities are being poked?

In 2011 alone, 1.2 million tons of imported chicken worth millions of dollars were dumped into the stomachs of millions of sub-Saharan Africans. There's also beef, fish, sausage, pork feet, and so many others that are imported into our markets. Our African societies and people are now so immersed in consumerism that we forget there was once pride in self-production. The backyard chicken farm of true African breed and the titillating aroma it gives when in the soup pot has vanished from the minds of my people.

Importation of food is not the problem. The problem is that our markets have become dumping grounds for all kinds of garbage called food. Some of these frozen meat has been frozen for years which raises serious health implications when consumed. The factory-style of producing meat undercuts the natural processes in the name of profits. Chicken eggs can be inserted in one section of their machines and within a few days' time, chicken meat is wrapped in another section. By the time it reaches our ports, it had gone through several cold stores and ships.

We did not only import joy to our sweet tooth but also sickness to the body. The new entrants to the latest top five causes of death, stroke and ischemic heart disease relate to what you eat into your body. Eat to live well, not eat to fill the belly. This is why Hippocrates believed that the body is made of four liquids namely blood, phlegm, yellow bile and black bile which require balance for the proper functioning of the organism. No matter how ancient this thought is, it underscores the fact that except one who was born sick, you can enjoy health if you are conscious of what you consume.

I daresay, not many are conscious of what they consume. Apart from food abuse, there's also drug abuse. Urbanization is truly an enigma, on the one hand, there's beauty - better social amenities and more distribution of wealth and the other hand holds debauchery. The rate at which our youth are consuming illicit drugs, the old ones and the recent cough syrups is alarming. Drug abuse is often accompanied by promiscuity, often on the blind side of the fact that HIV/AIDS exists.

Obesity has become celebratory in some parts of Africa that a man's wealth is measured by the size of his protruding belly. At least we know that until the arrival of the white man en masse, our people hadn't had a major shift in dietary for centuries. Surely this would have had some genetic bearing on our bodies and most importantly, metabolism. Metabolism is the process by which the body converts food into energy. When you eat more than your body needs, the unused energy which is sometimes more than the used one, is stored as fat in some portion of your body, quite latently.

Consumerism had rocked most parts of the world and was only gaining center stage in Africa, noticeably, by the beginning of the 21st century. Some have argued that it is an innocuous terminology that oils the wheels of capitalism. Because when you consume more, it is the capitalist who profits. But why talk about this under health? Because some of the articles of consumption debilitate health. So why yield to the popular culture to consume more of them?

The days when the best brands were well known and respected seems to be fleeting nowadays. The brands are many and most of them are unregulated. The myriad energy drinks, canned beer, pastries with weird labels, herbal mixtures, etc. deserve scrutiny before purchase. Sometimes, the expiry dates are written in Chinese, Turkish, Arabic, and other unreadable languages to the average

African. These products are abundant and every mindful person ought to admit it. It's as if the nicer the packaging of these imported foods the more entrenched the idea that the food it contains would be equally nice. And therefore not paying attention to the labels. Our regulators have to be more proactive to prevent the influx of unwholesome foods.

My friend's daughter had malaria a couple of weeks ago. By midnight of the first day of symptoms, the whole house was on alert because her condition had worsened but they kept their cool and used what little first aid they had at home until the morning. They did not bother to go to the closest hospital, which happens to be a government facility, because going to a government hospital at such odd hours is no guarantee of medical service.

In the morning when they got to the hospital, the queue was long and the doctors had not arrived yet. His prowess at analysis quickly informed him that his daughter's turn to see a doctor would be much later into the afternoon and so he worked out an alternative to go to a private practitioner. Those who did not have the luxury of seeing a private doctor had to endure all the discomfort of being in the queue unattended, and with whatever conditions they were suffering from. This was in the capital city.

The other day while going through the news, a picture with a headline saddened my day and stole my appetite for lunch that day. It was a picture of a pregnant woman in labor being transported to the hospital over 20 kilometers away on a motorbike along with her helper somewhere in the Kpandai District of Ghana.

Three people on a motorbike excluding the unborn child who was in a hurry to come into a world it knows nothing about. I don't know which concerned the unborn child more; whether the discomfort resulting from its mother being sandwiched between the rider and her helper or the potholes which bumped the motorcycle and made it all seem like a rollercoaster.

We repeat these examples so that our leaders would better appreciate the size of the load they carry. It is heavy but they must carry it well. It is erroneous for people to fixate their minds on politicians alone when they talk about leaders. There are business leaders in private practice who can change the world. There are religious leaders whose voices bring meaning to life. There are community leaders who galvanize their societies. There are many others including me and you who can participate in the process of making the world better.

Because of lack of knowledge my people suffer is a famous biblical text. Indeed, ignorance is a wicked affliction. It narrows your perspective and impassions your arguments. To reason with ignorance is to uproot it before proper understanding can occur. That is why more education is required to sensitize people on health consciousness aside the need, of course, to improve infrastructure.

CORRUPTION

I would like to start this section with a famous statement by the former president of Ghana, H.E. John Agyekum Kufuor, with no malice intended of course. He said corruption is as old as Adam, the first man. This statement was part of an answer he gave when he was asked about alleged corruption under his watch. There's a tendency to misunderstand people, I don't know whether it is sometimes deliberate or we are what the psychologists call cognitive misers. But it is true that corruption is as old as Adam, in a manner of speaking.

Man has a tendency to excuse himself of blame and so we shifted cause of our corruption to a serpent, the devil. Corruption, especially graft of the public purse is a reflection of the perpetrator's greediness, the serpent is long dead. A few individuals appropriating to themselves what is meant for the whole nation by virtue of their positions as public officials through dishonest means can be considered as an apt definition of the corruption that beset our development as African people.

Because of man's susceptibility to corruption, human societies the world over and throughout history have committed themselves to institutionalize measures to curb it. But in Africa, the commitment is not shared by all and thus the fight against corruption has not gained traction.

Earlier I made reference to the 2016 study by Transparency International which discovered that corruption is endemic in Africa. This was thirteen years after the African Union adopted a convention in Maputo on July 11, 2003 to "preventing and combating corruption". After I read through the lengthy document, it was immediately apparent to me that the AU is well versed in the issues of corruption in Africa. In fact, the preamble was enough to convince me that African leadership needs no further study of the menace, probably because it emanates from themselves. For the purpose of clarity, the preamble is included below:

African Union Convention on Preventing and Combating Corruption

PREAMBLE

The Member States of the African Union:

1. ***Considering*** *that the Constitutive Act of the African Union recognizes that freedom, equality, justice, peace and dignity are essential objectives for the achievement of the legitimate aspiration of the African peoples;*
2. ***Further considering*** *that Article 3 of the said Constitutive Act enjoins Member States to coordinate and intensify their cooperation, unity, cohesion and efforts to achieve a better life for the peoples of Africa;*
3. ***Cognizant*** *of the fact that the Constitutive Act of the African Union, inter alia, calls for the need to promote and protect human and peoples' rights, consolidate democratic institutions and foster a culture of democracy and ensure good governance and the rule of law;*
4. ***Aware*** *of the need to respect human dignity and to foster the promotion of economic, social, and political rights in conformity with the provisions of the African Charter on Human and People's Rights and other relevant human rights instruments;*

5. ***Bearing in mind*** *the 1990 Declaration on the Fundamental Changes Taking Place in the World and their Implications for Africa; the 1994 Cairo Agenda for Action Relaunching Africa's Socio-economic Transformation; and the Plan of Action Against Impunity adopted by the Nineteenth Ordinary Session of the African Commission on Human and Peoples Rights in 1996 as subsequently endorsed by the Sixty fourth Ordinary Session of the Council of Ministers held in Yaounde, Cameroon in 1996 which, among others, underlined the need to observe principles of good governance, the primacy of law, human rights, democratization and popular participation by the African peoples in the processes of governance.*
6. ***Concerned*** *about the negative effects of corruption and impunity on the political, economic, social and cultural stability of African States and its devastating effects on the economic and social development of the African peoples;*
7. ***Acknowledging*** *that corruption undermines accountability and transparency in the management of public affairs as well as socio-economic development on the continent;*
8. ***Recognizing*** *the need to address the root causes of corruption on the continent;*
9. ***Convinced*** *of the need to formulate and pursue, as a matter of priority, a common penal policy aimed at*

protecting the society against corruption, including the adoption of appropriate legislative and adequate preventive measures;

10. ***Determined** to build partnerships between governments and all segments of civil society, in particular, women, youth, media and the private sector in order to fight the scourge of corruption;*
11. ***Recalling** resolution AHG-Dec 126(XXXIV) adopted by the Thirty–fourth Ordinary Session of the Assembly of Heads of State and Government in June 1998 in Ouagadougou, Burkina Faso, requesting the Secretary General to convene, in cooperation with the African Commission on Human and Peoples' Rights, a high level meeting of experts to consider ways and means of removing obstacles to the enjoyment of economic, social and cultural rights, including the fight against corruption and impunity and propose appropriate legislative and other measures;*
12. ***Further recalling** the decision of the 37th ordinary session of the Assembly of Heads of State and Government of the OAU held in Lusaka, Zambia, in July 2001 as well as the Declaration adopted by the first session of the Assembly of the Union held in Durban, South Africa in July 2002, relating to the New Partnership for Africa's Development (NEPAD) which calls for the setting up of a coordinated mechanism to combat corruption effectively.*

All twelve sections of the preamble begin with strong words and have clearly highlighted the AU's deep understanding of the issues of corruption and therefore adopted the convention which details various acts of corruption and proscribes stringent methods for dealing with the menace.

Fairly speaking the AU's convention marked a milestone in the fight against corruption in Africa. Subsequently, and even before, member States of the AU have implemented many anti-corruption programmes but somehow the canker still stares us gleefully in the face.

AU's Heads of States and Governments declared the year 2018 as "Africa Anticorruption Year", I believe this move was meant to increase its sensitization of anticorruption efforts on the continent but barely half of the year 2018 has passed and one of the crocodiles in the pond comes out to resign while accusing the AU's Advisory Board on Corruption of corruption. Mr. Daniel Batidam, until 8th June, 2018 was a board member of AU's anticorruption unit, AUABC. He held that position for three years, having been re-elected in 2017 to serve his second and last two-year term.

In his letter to the chairperson of AUABC, the Hon. Begoto Miarom, Mr. Batidam stated that, "After witnessing several instances and degrees of bad governance, including the abuse of entrusted power (or corruption), lack of probity, accountability, transparency and integrity at the Secretariat of the AUABC and some Departments of the AU Commission itself for over a period of three years now, while efforts at seeking redress have yielded no results, I have decided on grounds of principle that enough is enough,".

There is a proverb that, when a crocodile comes out of the pond to tell you what goes on in the pond, you'd be remiss not to believe it. Although Mr. Batidam's claims are yet to be proven, they buttress the perception that is already widely held.

The AU estimated in a 2002 study that corruption costs Africa $ 150 billion a year which belittles the average yearly Official Development Assistance (ODA) or foreign aid given to sub-Saharan Africa. For instance, it was reported that in 2008, ODA to sub-Saharan Africa was $ 22.5 billion, thus, emboldening the fact that, if SSA were triumphant in its fight against corruption, it would not need foreign aid.

How can we understand how corruption thrives in SSA in spite of its illegality across the continent? Behaviorists have said that a bad behavior festers if there is no punishment but that is not the case here. There is punishment for corruption – when the perpetrator is caught. So why is corruption still on the surge?

How do we stop something that is so deeply woven into our social and psychological lives? For as far as I can remember my life as an African, influencing people with material things, especially money is a daily life encounter. We don't discriminate, we love giving and we love taking.

How do we change the ideological perspective of a person whose only motivation is amassing wealth and living large, where living large means building mansions and filling them with luxury cars, unbridled libido and dancing and throwing money at funerals?

How do we get our president to understand that when his nephew, who is holding public office is culpable of some corruption charges, he'd follow due process because it is in the interest of the public to do so? How do we reshape the psychology of a public official who has made a deal with a contractor to overprice a project? How do we erect the morals of that police officer to promulgate justice for that young girl who was raped, against any inducement to corruption?

But most importantly, how do we ingrain in the public a high sense of abhorrence for all acts of corruption? How do we build strong public opinion against corruption such that a mere suspicion would be enough to smoke out a rat from its hole of public office? I don't mean the Ghanaian condition where we talk and go to sleep, no, that is not what I mean. The public have to make themselves so fearful that when someone thinks of committing corruption, the maiden thought of public uproar would make their stomach cringe.

When shall a group of people, being moved by anger for their disdain for corruption, organize themselves to go to court every time and follow court proceedings on a case that involves their District Chief Executive for embezzlement? How do we cultivate the mentality to be vigilant at all times to watch over the watchman and bring justice to ourselves?

Public opinion here has reminded me of the concept, "divide and rule". In most Sub-Saharan countries, the case may not be too far from the Ghanaian case where two leading political parties rotate power. Over the past, voting statistics suggest that they each have a core support base of at least 40% of voters (by extension the public). So at any time, public opinion is shared almost equally by two leading political parties. If someone is accused of corruption and he belongs to one party, the general response from that party and especially their followers, would be to defend the accused and state that it is witch-hunting from the other party.

People sometimes reason below or above logic to defend their party fellow even in the glaring face of truth.

Things like this do hamper the formation of strong public opinion against corruption. An enduring public opinion is required in the delivery of justice. When public interest is lowered on a case, the justice delivery apparatus malfunctions; and whose fault would it be?

The World Bank estimated in a 2003 report that the average cost of building a classroom in Africa was 7,000 dollars. If this amount is still valid and if President Muhammadu Buhari would be kind enough to donate the $9.1 billion looted money his government recovered from its anti-corruption campaign, Africa's education would be boosted by 1.3 million classrooms. A few people of high places decided to keep all that money to themselves. And as usual to live large, without recourse to the perpetual misery the poor majority are subjected to.

President Muhammadu Buhari is old and not so healthy, I pray to Allah for his health, but with his dedication to fighting the rot, he is marking a significant juncture in the trajectory of the fight against corruption in Africa's most populous and leading economy, Nigeria. With his results, I wonder what a younger man, filled with vim and vigor and castrated of all corruption tendencies, would do. Such is the politics of Africa, the old men don't want to go away and the youth are helpless.

President Muhammadu Buhari is not alone, when President John Magufuli took power in November 2015, it was clear from the onset that corruption and government profligacy would not receive oxygen in his government. He rolled out many austerity measures to deal with the unbridled spending of public monies which successive Tanzanian (or African) governments are known for. He reduced his salary by more than 70 per cent amongst other austere measures notably; suspending Tanzania's 2015 Independence Day festivities to carry out a nationwide cleanup exercise which he, himself bent down and picked rubbish.

His resolve is underscored by his decisiveness and devotion to action. No man is without blame but I hope that Magufuli's blame would not be about corruption. I hope that his blame would not be one of the fundamental problems of Africa – the one-man show. I hope that he is just trying to do his best to contributing his quota to shape the system for a better tomorrow.

But while all this may be so, it should not surprise anyone to eavesdrop on some of Magufuli's presidential colleagues and friends, conversing and laughing about him, for being a fool to leave a juicy pie to rot. If I were him, I would quote Mathew chapter four verse four of the Bible to such 'stomach politicians' and make them understand that others too deserve the pie. I find that whenever someone dares to tackle the ills of society with such boisterous resolve, the system ostracizes them because some people are more comfortable with the ills. We pray for more Magufulis but that would not be possible without Magufuli himself standing the test of time.

Earlier I stated that corruption is a cultural problem but I guess, that is ubiquitous across human cultures. It is when the fight against corruption hits a cultural roadblock, that, the real danger looms. The cultural problem of tribalism has dealt a serious blow to the fight against corruption. Being proud of your tribe is not the same as projecting it above others. I am proud of my tribe but the point is, I needn't even say it because everybody is proud of theirs.

One main area tribalism begins to destroy things is the arena of political parties. Party politics seems to be conjoined with democracy but is it not party politics that divides the people into factions fighting each other? We should not say that the factions are good for comparing ideas because any group of people when acting in unity will make the best decisions for themselves. Democracy then loses its ideal flavour, isn't it? Considering that democracy is the best we've had and political parties are its mainstays, what can we do to stripe parties of tribalism, and especially, partisan loyalism against public interest? Such a herculean task who can do?

The media is a crucial element of the mix to fighting corruption but word from the grapevine has it that, some media houses are either owned or funded by politicians. Which raises serious concerns because media attention on a matter of national interest may be polarized along party lines.

However, the days when people relied on a few media organizations are over. The Internet and social media have broadened journalism which is making it possible for the dissipation of the boundaries that once obfuscated information dissemination. The high penetration of such platforms throughout the continent is indicative of people power; to enable us as Africans to crowdsource ideas on development, and also to consolidate public opinion and pressure on our leaders.

As I write, there are many other writers and bloggers who are reshaping the African narrative through these new media platforms. Despite the potential of these new technologies, the nemesis of progress lurks around us. Some governments in SSA have made legislative moves to put a tighter leash on the use of social media to once again, control information. President Yoweri Museveni was not remiss at all when he announced that his government plans to tax Ugandans for their use of social media to curb what he calls gossip.

It is some of these new technologies that is empowering resilient journalists such as Anas Aremeyaw

Anas who is bringing innovation and conviction in the fight against corruption across the continent. Anas' hard work in 2014 brought cataclysmic changes in the Judiciary of Ghana. Highly-placed personalities within Ghana's Judiciary were caught live on camera taking bribes to 'fart over justice', so to speak.

Before the Judiciary, Anas exposed a massive network of corrupt Customs officials and clearing agents operating at Ghana's Ports and Harbors Authority. His investigations have caught many fishes but none was as big as the President of the Ghana Football Association (GFA). He, together with over a hundred football officials within and outside the GFA were captured by Anas' secret filming cameras taking various sums of money to fix one thing or the other. In the Anas footages, almost everyone who was approached acquiesced to bribery without any appreciable apprehension. Suggestive of a cultural mindset.

When nobody sees nothing wrong with corruption, it only becomes culpable when you are caught. But those who are supposed to catch the thieves, bemoan of weak systems. What is direr is that, they are most likely corrupt themselves. So here we are, being perpetually cloaked in this destructive cycle.

There seems to be a general acceptance of the existence of corruption which underscores how deep it is entrenched in our psyches. A child today in Ghana knows very well about corruption. If you are exposed to it from such young age and continually develop to accept that you can get away with corruption, you'd automatically be corruptible because the proceeds of corruption are lucrative.

So lucrative that people risk it all to partake in it. Kwesi Nyantakyi, now former President of the Ghana Football Association, was cruising in a comfortable trajectory to becoming an affable member of the top hierarchy of FIFA. Because of his appearance in the Anas expose number 12, bagging sums of dollars, his flamboyant career in football administration has now sunk below the devil's belt through a bottomless ditch leading nowhere.

I hope I am not guilty of the "pull-him-down" syndrome plaguing Africa but how could I be when the man was caught live on camera? This is how bold our leaders have become with respect to corruption. We too ought to be bold.

One day in 2015, the world woke up to a shocking arson. It was the Central Medical Stores of Ghana which houses medical supplies meant for distribution to the whole nation. According to some kind estimates, medical items amounting to $80 million were gutted in the fire which investigation proved to be arson.

The US Ambassador to Ghana, Mr. Robert Jackson in August 2017 during the Ghana Good Corporate Governance Initiative roundtable event in Accra, lamented about the arson - "After two years, we are still waiting for justice in the CMS (central medical stores) arson. The fire destroyed more than $80 million worth of medical supplies and drugs, including $7 million in donations provided by the American people…This fire, which was ignited to cover up corruption, dealt a significant blow to public health in Ghana".

Former UK High Commissioner to Ghana, Jon Benjamin also spoke of the arson - "In the Central Medical

Stores, there were 4 million pounds worth of medicines bought by the UK through our DFID programme that were there and were destroyed and we had to account for that money and questions were asked in the UK Parliament. So we had to say what had happened and what was being done about it."

Some shady network of people didn't want the government to discover the rot in the CMS and so they set fire to it to erase the evidence. Twelve persons were interdicted from the Ghana Health Service but this cannot remedy the loss the nation suffered. Apart from the $80 million worth of medical supplies and drugs, there was massive damage to the facility and its premises, also amounting to several million dollars. The nation had already been grappling with meager resources for healthcare, the arson therefore created a dire shortage of medical supplies across the nation. The full extent of the arson as well as its collateral damages may never be known. And yet this is just a tip of the iceberg of the damages of corruption.

FLEEING THE CONTINENT

Sub-Saharan Africa is the largest region of the world where migrants are most welcomed. On the flip side, migrants from SSA suffer the most migration restrictions. This is more so for unskilled migrants but generally, it is easy for an American to migrate to Ghana but the opposite is not true. It is easy for a Chinese to migrate to Djibouti but the opposite is not true. It is easy for a Lebanese to migrate to Liberia, but a Liberian would have to prove beyond his ability before he'd be granted migration permit to enter Lebanon. This is all true.

Migration dates back to the earliest times because hunting and gathering requires a lot of moving around. Today, for almost the same reasons, we are still moving around to better one thing or the other.

Migration is often the automatic result of deficiency. When there's deficit of jobs, people migrate to other areas where they believe there are jobs. Where there's deficit of peace, people migrate to live in peace. When there's deficit of food, people move. When people feel a deficit of the full complement of their human rights, the result is no different, they'd migrate if the opportunity exists, and it should. For example, if a Ghanaian were to have some deficit and plan to migrate to America, it should be easy but the problem is that, America too, as a nation must want to vet him or her on some standards which naturally, there's eighty per cent chance that they'd fail.

And that is the story of millions of sub-Saharan Africans who apply for Visas every year. When you apply you'd not get it unless you are one who can polish your teeth as white as snow to meet their requirements. Despite the difficulties, the wish to flee the continent is pervasive among Africa's desperate youth.

Growing up in the eighties and nineties, one thing was clear amongst me and my peers, "go Yankee or London". Only a small fraction of the hopefuls got to realize their dreams. Our motivation was simply to get better life and no matter how hard we tried to convince ourselves, we still believed there was better life outside the shores of Africa. I feel sad that after all these years the situation has rather multiplied negatively. Worse is that, people are still having to pay the ultimate price to flee the continent.

Forty-four Ghanaians are now resting peacefully in the bosom of Hades because they were trying to get to Libya by road, from where they wished to travel to Europe but were brutally murdered by the 'Junglers', a paramilitary squad which operated at the beck and call of former President of the Gambia, Yahya Jammeh. They mistook the migrants for mercenaries sent to oust Yahya Jammeh. It wasn't only Ghanaians, there were a few Nigerians, Senegalese and Togolese, all embarking on the journey to the West. One person survived whom I suspect is now a repentant migrant but I'm not sure because the wish to flee Africa abounds.

The lone survivor was lucky indeed. In a media encounter organized by the Centre for Democratic Development (CDD-Ghana) in Accra, Mr. Martin Kyere narrated the ordeal he endured to escape. Fate may have given him a second chance because somebody had to tell their story. But the effect we would have hoped for from telling such a story is not being gained, many more embark on the journey away from Africa through such perilous channels.

The United Nations agency for migration, the International Organization for Migration (IOM) is one of the busiest agencies of the UN. One of its busiest flashpoints is the Mediterranean area, where poverty and war are pushing thousands of Africans through a pendulous swing of fate to escape the continent.

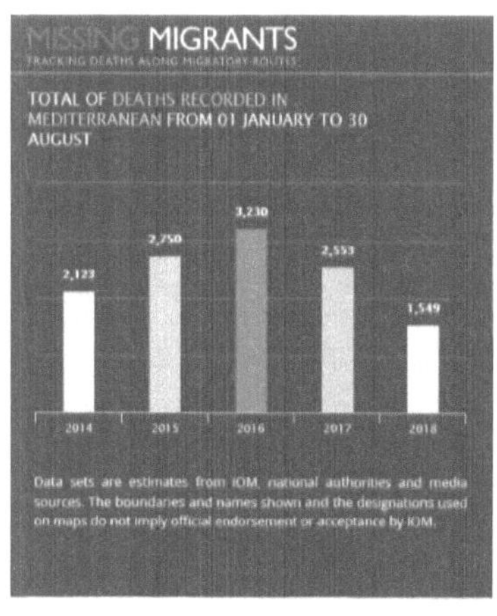

From IOM website

Between 2014 and August 2018, about 12,205 deaths have occurred in the three main migration routes in the area; Central Mediterranean, Eastern Mediterranean and Western Mediterranean. "Attempted crossings" which according to the International Organization for Migration (IOM) "include sea arrivals in Spain, Italy, Cyprus, and Greece, land arrivals in Spain, and interceptions by the Tunisian National Guard and Turkish and Libyan Coast Guards" is much more in number compared with the number of deaths.

In the immediate past year 2017, there were 111, 968 attempted crossings. Meaning death rate for that year was 2.1%. But this 2.1% excludes those who might have died or captured by terrorists en route to the Mediterranean.

The danger with illegal migration or should we say, 'desperate migration' from Africa does not begin on the Mediterranean waters. Traveling by road to Libya is perilous. And even more so for women and children. Al-Qaeda, Al-Shabaab and Boko Haram are just a few of the terrorist groups that operate in the region and one of their methods of recruitment is by taking captives. Migrants also run the risk of being victimized by banditry which results in their total loss of personal effects and possibly, lives.

Africa's democracy, no matter how infant, should by now have provided the kind of leadership that is needed to solve our problems because our problems are grave indeed. Otherwise, how is it understandable that a young boy from Bangui, fleeing from war, would find himself making the decision to embark a rickety boat in the Mediterranean; knowing fully well, it is either cross or die crossing? Whereas crossing is no guarantee of anything except that it is better than his homeland, Africa.

It should perhaps not be a big deal at all that the narrative of Africa would include the desperate manner in which her children crave fleeing away from her dusty overcrowded cities and lifeless hinterlands. But we have to acknowledge the power of high-capacity manpower to solve our development challenges, against the reality that the West continues to poach Africa's bright youngsters.

There is a huge challenge in the manpower dynamics of Sub-Saharan Africa. A situation that is similar to how raw materials are exported outside SSA market at low cost and the importation of value-added goods. There's a great deal of brain drain that is heavily undercutting Africa's development. Her teeming youth are forced to find pasture elsewhere amid her overflowing fountain of wealth, or rather untapped wealth. The tapping of which is unscrupulously mismanaged.

Jobs are changing and becoming more specialized and technology based. However, the educational apparatuses of Africa do not fully support the development of highly qualified technocrats in certain fields which are critical for the current and future dynamics of jobs. This means that, the percentage of local content who occupy certain high-capacity driven jobs is reducing and being filled with expats. Manpower is no doubt one of Africa's biggest import services which also no doubt is at the expense of her youth.

The lack of jobs and the rising cost of living is forcing millions to yearn to travel out and hope for better future. The cities are becoming more cosmopolitan and less conducive to the poor, whose marginalization is spelling doom.

Rising population is also accountable for the emigration crisis of Africa. This winding and unwinding pattern of Africa's future should be of serious concern to us all. Our governments are almost hamstrung with current figures of populations; the situation will be much direr by 2050 when it has been projected that Africa will have added 1.3 billion more people to its current population. That's just three decades from now.

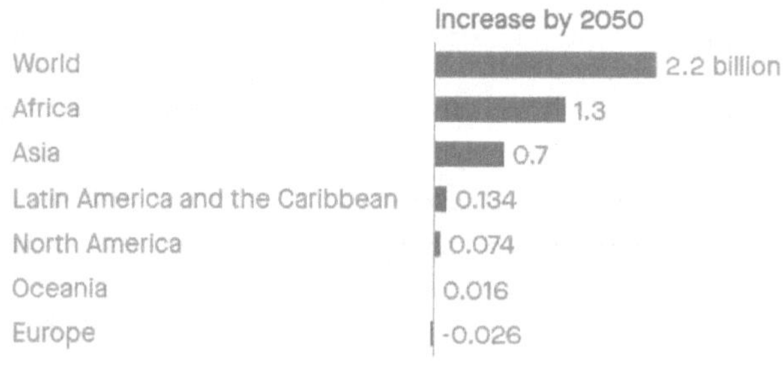

Despite the apparent urgency of the situation, not much is being done in preparation to offset the existential population crises. Nigeria will be worst hit according to the statistics and I hope the Nigerian government is taking serious cognizance of these facts. At present, Nigeria's population, combined with its meek and bleak economic performance is what is fueling its security issues; having to do with terrorism, kidnapping, human trafficking, etc. In 30 years' time, its population will more than double and if proactive policies are not properly implemented, so will Nigeria's problems.

Population growth is no doubt one of the causes of unemployment. The high unemployment rate is also keeping Africa's talent away in their sojourn from returning home and contributing to the development of their homeland. There are thousands of Africa's human resources who are forced by circumstances to not return home. Simply because our governments do not have a fair system in place to absorb their reintegration which is often difficult because they have been away for too long.

Shouldn't it be a plus for us if our brothers and sisters in the Diaspora decide to return and offer their expertise? Especially through a programme that is equitably dispensed, rather than the partisan politics that the issue has been marred with?

www.ingramcontent.com/pod-product-compliance
Lightning Source LLC
Chambersburg PA
CBHW051310250726
48656CB00004B/1588